Memoirs and More

A Father's Legacy

Marvin LeRoy Oed

PublishAmerica
Baltimore

© 2009 by Marvin LeRoy Oed.
All rights reserved. No part of this book may be reproduced, stored in a retrieval system or transmitted in any form or by any means without the prior written permission of the publishers, except by a reviewer who may quote brief passages in a review to be printed in a newspaper, magazine or journal.

First printing

PublishAmerica has allowed this work to remain exactly as the author intended, verbatim, without editorial input.

ISBN: 978-1-60749-354-9
PUBLISHED BY PUBLISHAMERICA, LLLP
www.publishamerica.com
Baltimore

Printed in the United States of America

DEDICATION

To my wife Lois who came into my life when we were in high school and has been, "Where I was when…" ever since.

ACKNOWLEDGMENTS

To: Those who had the greatest influence on who I became.

My grandparents, Philip Jacob and Eleanor Emge Dannenfelser, I lived with my grandparents from the time I was two years old until I married. They were, "Where I was when…" for about twenty years.

My parents, Benjamin Leroy and Leona Dannenfelser Oed
I lived with my parents from birth until I married. They were, "Where I was when…" for twenty-two years.

All the many others who influenced my life.

FOREWORD

Memories fade with time. The facts are accurate, at least as I remember them. This was spell and grammar checked by Microsoft Office Word, not professionally reviewed. Therefore, I take the responsibility for all spelling, grammatical, and punctuation errors as well as political incorrectness. Some are intentional. When the gender is unclear or includes both male and female, the masculine is used. This may now be politically incorrect. I learned this way and it never caused me any problems. To use he/she and him/her is unwieldy, unnecessary and just plain silly.

In *"What You Are Now Is Where You Were When..."* Sociologist Morris Massey wrote that, "We perceive events in the context in which we experience them." This determines what we perceive as truth. People and events provide the foundation for our perceptions of what we have seen, heard and experienced. From this, we each create our own reality. The truth is that reality does not exist. What we perceive as truth is our reality.

Many philosophers say, "You become what you think about." This takes Massey's concept a step further. Perceptions change. As our perceptions change, our reality changes and as our reality changes our thinking changes. The changes are not clear-cut. Psychologists say that most often we see what we're told to see, what we want to see and even what we're afraid of seeing. Almost all philosophers will agree that how we think and what we think about most is what we become.

My parents and grandparents had the greatest impact on me as a young child. As I grew, historical events, education, peers, colleagues, etc. added their influence. The combination of people, pertinent historical events and the context in which I experienced them made me what I am. Genes my determine traits initially, however, life experiences modify them.

The process of writing required me to look at my life in a way I never had before. The more I wrote the more I learned about myself. I am proud of some of the things I have done and not proud of others. Do I have regrets? To me the word regret infers some ongoing distress or disappointment regarding what I did or said in the past. Everyone has twenty-twenty hindsight. Yes, there are things I know I should have done differently. However, life does not permit "do overs." As much as I might like to, I cannot change the past. In addition, dwelling on the past gains one nothing.

"Everyman has three Characters, that Which he exhibits, that which has and That which he thinks he is."
Alphonse Karr

Most memoirs focus on what an individual did. Accomplishments can be important yet tell little about the person. What makes me what I am, is the result of a myriad of events that occurred over my lifetime. Some events are remembered and others forgotten but m a result of the combination of all these events. In *"Memoirs and More"* I attempt to go "behind the scenes" and share my experiences in the light of my upbringing, my way of thinking, my attitudes, my beliefs, my feelings and my experiences. This is where I developed into me.

"The only constant is change, continuing change…"
Isaac Asimov

What we are began with genes. What we become is the result of our perception of the events we experience and the people we encounter throughout life. Genes determine traits initially. In a never-ending process, life experiences modify them. My parents were the first people who influenced me. However, there is no way of knowing how far in the past a characteristic of theirs may have originated. They also were a product of the influence of their parents and experiences, as were their parents before them, etc.

PROLOGUE

The boy in a typical Horatio Alger story always overcame a myriad of hardships and difficulties in order to achieve his life-long dream. Were this me, my memoirs would describe my vision of the "American Dream" and the hardships and misfortunes I overcame before achieving my dream. This would make me a role model for others to emulate. That would make a good story, but would not be my story. It's not even close. My successes have been in spite of, rather than because of, insightful planning and preparation. This worked for me, yet I would not recommend it to others.

The first and only time I thought about what I was going to do in life was for a few minutes in junior high school. My teacher asked that we choose a profession or line of work that interested us. I never thought about this before. I chose draftsman, only because shop was the only class that I enjoyed and I especially enjoyed mechanical drawing. All I really wanted was to get from one grade to the next and get out. I frequently heard that once out of school I would wish to be back. That has never happened. I did not like elementary school, I did not like junior high school, I did not like high school and I did not like college. I always liked working much more than I ever liked school.

"If you don't know where you're going,
you'll end up someplace else"
Yogi Berra

Thinking about a career, setting a goal or selecting a role model to emulate never crossed my mind.

My career was a journey without a destination. That is the way I wanted it. There is more joy in the effort than there is in the attainment. There was no need to set a goal. I had a job to do; my to-do list reminded me of what needed I needed to do. What Yogi Berra said in jest worked fine for me. I was always ready to change directions. However, when I wanted to be somewhere else, exactly where was not important.

My objective is always to implement processes and procedures that improve efficiency, effectiveness, etc. Once everything works well, it becomes time to move on to something different. It would be a mistake for me to believe that what I like and want to do today will be the same tomorrow. After doing something for a length of time I find I would rather be doing something else.

I had no reason to choose pharmacy school other that I knew I wanted (my parents said had) to go to college. I never gave any thought to career planning. During a Sunday lunch with my parents in the Copper Kettle restaurant, my father mentioned his friend who was a pharmacist and had retired at age fifty-five. Retiring early sounded good and I had nothing against pharmacy. I applied immediately. The highly structured curriculum of the school of pharmacy was good for me because it automatically provided a general career direction.

My career developed as perceived opportunities arose. I made choices rapidly and never looked back. The outcome of a decision never determines whether the decision is good or bad. If the decision is reasonable based upon the information available at the time, the decision is good, regardless of the outcome. Good and bad frequently change. What seems good initially may seem bad later and even later appear to be good again. Rarely is there a way to know the outcome of an option not chosen. My choice of pharmacy school was "bad" in the sense that no thought was involved but "good" in the sense that it worked out well. My philosophy for life and poker is the same. Stick with what looks good, throw in what looks bad and do not agonize over the outcome. It is probably a good thing that I only play penny-ante poker. Incongruously, at pharmacy school, I attended, and later taught, a seminar on how to make appropriate pharmacy career decisions. We all use a combination of thinking, feeling and action in the decision process. All are important. Over or under emphasizing one aspect leads to irrational conclusions. Facts are necessary; however, over-thinking leads to indecision. Consider personal feelings (intuition), but never make them the sole determinant. Acting without sufficient thought and not considering feelings can lead to disaster. Doing nothing is a decision also. I learned that I am very much a doer and very little a feeler. Not considering how I would feel afterward led to some misguided decisions. What career would I have chosen had I given it more thought? I have no idea. Students often asked me which of my jobs I liked the most. My teasing answer was, "The one I haven't had yet." My explanation was that I liked them all but look forward to doing something different.

I have no need for long-term goals. I live in the present and never in the past or future. I always worked hard and did my best so I feel I was ambitious. Rather than a goal, I had a to-do list. I was always willing to try something new or quick to adopt and adapt innovations as they appeared.

The "Great Depression" resulted in a long, difficult period for a great number of people throughout the world. The 1920's was a decade of peace, prosperity and euphoria until the stock market crashed in 1929. Many blamed the banks for their losses and many viewed criminals such as Dillinger, Baby Face Nelson, and Machine Gun Kelly as heroes and their bank robberies as a fitting payback. Compounding the problem was a nine-year drought that began in the mid-west in the year 1930. Farmers' fields literally blew away because the ground was so dry. Two and a half million people migrated, many losing their farms, some able to take only what they could carry.

My father worked for his father and took over the store when his father died. The store must have had a name, but I never heard it called anything other than, *"the store."* Those fortunate enough to have jobs often earned little money. When short on cash, they would run a tab (no credit cards then) at *the store*. When customers had cash, rather than patronize my father, they would go to a chain store where prices were lower. This is understandable for people doing their best to make ends meet, but make it impossible to sustain a business. I heard this story several times, however I never once heard my father complain or criticize this behavior. These were tough times and people did what they had to do to survive. My father gave the store to his brother (Uncle George) who ran the business for a while. After the store closed, Uncle George lived there with his sister (Aunt Thelma) and her husband (Uncle Louis) and their children. After they moved, it became a barbershop. In my teens, I had my hair cut there for $.50 during the week. If I waited until Saturday, it cost $.75.

Except for a period during World War II when my father worked for The Glenn L. Martin Company in Middle River, the only full-time position he ever held was that of paper cutter. Although offered promotions and other higher paying jobs he always turned them down. It was not a lack of ambition. My father always worked very hard, often working a second job part time. I believe my work ethic came from him. He was happy with his job and saw no need for status. What he did was satisfying to him; he did it well and was able to support his family. There was no need for anything more. He would come home livid when a supervisor accepted a less than perfect job. It was clear he was more upset at the supervisor who accepted poor work than the man who did it. I have similar feelings about shoddy workmanship. This is why I believe that success should be defined by how well you perform your job and how content you are rather than what position you hold, how much money you make or what possessions you have. By that definition, he was as successful as anyone I ever met.

My mother liked working at a job better than housework. She held a variety of full and part time positions while I was growing up. Since my grandmother was there, I never came home to an empty house.

My mother had a somewhat different outlook than my father. She aspired to move to a "better" (Overlea was not bad) neighborhood, live in a larger house and associate with those who held more prestigious positions or higher paying jobs. She would have preferred that my father have a "position" rather than a "job." She may have even felt some embarrassment that her husband was "only" a working-man. Looking back, I wonder how this made him feel. He, I am much like him, was never one to react noticeably so if something bothered him no one would know. My mother said she only knew something was wrong when he just stopped talking to her. I was never aware of this. However, I am oblivious to most of the nuances in people's behavior. When she joined the Woman's Club of Towson, it bothered her knowing that that the members would see her 21206 (Overlea) zip code listed in their handbook. I suspect my father could not have cared less. It pleased my mother when they moved to an apartment and the zip code in the handbook changed to 21204 (Towson).

The depression was at its worst during 1933-1935. Franklin Roosevelt was president and the programs instituted at the time began getting people back to work. The reality of a war in Europe was increasing. As a result, the economy began to improve. I was too young to have any direct recollection of the depression, but those, such as my parents, who lived through it, never forgot. Many people lost their jobs and their homes and went hungry. We were more fortunate. My father had a job and earned enough money to get by. There is no question but the depression influenced my parents thinking regarding how they spent money and the need to save money for the rest of their lives.

Traits I saw in my parents and grandparents I now see in myself. Neither my parents nor grandparents were outwardly emotional or expressive about their feelings. There was little hugging or kissing. As far as I can remember, no one ever said, "I love you." I never felt unloved because I knew they loved me. I never saw any of them really cry. My father came close during his mother's funeral. I thought everyone was like this until I met Lois and her family. Lois, who I later married, was the first person I said, "I love you, too." It was fifty years later when I said it to a second person, my mother. This was at Lois' behest when my mother began having health issues due to aging. It's still not easy for me to say, "I love you," even to my children. I love them very much, but seldom express it. I do not feel that I missed anything by not hearing those words and hope that my kids don't.

Douglas stopped by for dinner one night. As he left, he and Lois kissed and each said, "I love you." I said my goodbye from the table. Lois said, "Get up here and give him a hug." I did. Maybe, with Lois encouraging me, I can change. Gregory and Leslie always kiss and hug Lois. Gregory and I always shake hands. Gregory taught me the man hug. We shake with the right hand while putting the left around the other's shoulder.

I'm becoming more used to, but am still uncomfortable with the kissing and hugging that has become common among friends. I would be just as happy to shake hands. In this aspect, I guess I am still a work in progress

Actions have greater influence than words. That must be how I learned right and wrong. My parents or grandparents never said, "Don't cheat, don't steal, don't lie, be courteous, don't talk back, etc." They didn't have to; I knew what was expected.

THE EARLY YEARS—
GROWING UP IN OVERLEA

I was born in Overlea, a suburb of Baltimore, in 1934. This was a gentler, more civil time. There was respect shown to, if there was not agreement with, parents, grandparents, teachers, police, employers, and adults in general. Unless they were friends, even adults addressed other adults as Mr., Mrs., or Miss. Even in college, professors called me Mr. Oed. I still shudder when I get a telephone call and someone who does not know me asks to speak to "Marvin." Children never addressed adults by their first name. I still believe it is inappropriate for a child to address any adult by first name.

"It's an ill wind that blows no good"
Anon.

Although the depression, an ill wind if there ever was one, had not ended, this was a good time to grow up in Overlea. I was too young to remember the depression. However, because of my parents' experiences, I learned that instant gratification is not important. The important things are to have a job, to save at least a little from each pay and to not buy anything if I do not have the money.

My mother's scrapbook includes a birth announcement. Marvin LeRoy Oed was born in the Raspeburg Maternity Hospital at the corner of Belair Road and White Avenue at 7:50 PM on September 27, 1934, a fair, warm day. I weighed eight pounds and eight ounces and had blue eyes and blond hair. In a short time, both the blue eyes and blonde hair became brown.

MARVIN LEROY OED

My father took over the grocery store in 1932 after his father died. My parents moved into the apartment above the store at Kenwood and Greenwood Avenues. I was born two years later. My recollection of the store is very dim. This is what I think I remember. There was a refrigerated meat case across the rear, wooden bins with slanted lids for bulk foods on one side and floor to ceiling shelves on the other. There was a tool to get items from shelves too high to reach. It was similar to, but longer than, the pick-ups now used to reach things on the floor. It also had two grips instead of one to close the grabbers. Overlea was still rural so the store sold animal feed, meat and groceries.

Currently In my living room is a long clock (grandmother clock) that I recall hearing as far back as I can remember. Now, when it chimes I think of my childhood on Elmont Avenue. The clock belonged to my grandparents, was passed on to my parents and then to me. So far, I have not been able to find any like it. I learned it is a mission style and that the Gilbert Company made the movement in 1910.

I walked from the store to visit my grandparents. I was very young; there would be a telephone call beforehand. My grandmother would watch down Elmont Ave toward Kenwood and my mother would watch up Kenwood Avenue toward Elmont to make certain I made it safely. I always did.

Before I began first grade we moved into an apartment in my grandparents' home at 1 Elmont Avenue. My grandfather converted the second floor into an apartment by adding a kitchen on the second floor and converting the attic into two rooms. My grandparents' apartment was on the first floor. Our apartment was above. A kitchen dining room, living room, my parents' bedroom and the bathroom was on the second floor. The two rooms in the attic were mine. I was a kid with a mini-apartment. The coal furnace was adapted to use oil before we moved in. However, the central heating did not reach the attic. Heat was from a kerosene stove at the bottom of the attic steps. As a safety precaution, my parents turned the stove off before they went to bed. Boy, could it get cold. On very cold days, I'd grab my clothing, run downstairs and dress in the living room. Later my grandfather added a radiator in the attic. There were no home air conditioners at that time. The only cooling in the summer was a window fan. Boy, could it get hot. In hot weather, I'd sleep on the front porch. Security was not the issue it is today. The lock on the screen door was just a simple latch. If no one was home when I came from school, I "unlocked" the screen door by lifting the latch with a stiff piece of paper. People went to the movies just to get out on the heat. Many theaters advertised they were air conditioned with large "It's Cool Inside" signs.

My grandfather built a rock garden with stones from the collapsed wall of a barn on a relative's family farm (Linden Farm) in Perry Hall. I made trips with him to the farm to bring the stones home in the back seat of his car. What a job! Imagine how many trips this must have required. He also brought a dozen or so small cedar trees from the farm that he planted as a backdrop for the rock garden. One tree never grew any taller and became my tree. In 1956, when Lois and I married, it was still only about four feet tall. The other trees were taller than the house.

In the center of the rock garden is a small pond. My grandfather bought lilies and put them in the pond. Fish eggs, in the lilies when he bought them, hatched. The fish survived the winters, sometimes frozen in the ice that formed. When the ice thawed, so did the fish. Most seemed no worse for their ordeal.

Although the pool was very small, I sometimes used it as a swimming pool. Two in the pool was a crowd. No one had home air conditioners at that time so the favorite way to cool off on days was to run under a lawn sprinkler.

My best friend at the time was Kenny Marshall. This was during World War II. We both wore army pilot's style hats. Knickers and military clothing were fashionable.

My grandfather also owned the empty lot next door. He made this his vegetable garden for a number of years. I often helped him plant. Every spring, a man from McCormick Avenue would bring his mule to plow the garden. His mule also provided the fertilizer. The odor was bad, but the fresh vegetables were good. My grandmother would can the vegetables for use during the winter. At the rear of this lot was a huge oak tree. Under the tree were a picnic table and benches my grandfather built. My father made a charcoal grill for cookouts.

Elmont Avenue was one long block that began at Kenwood Avenue and ended at a large piece of property owned by the McCormick Family. The log homes they built are still there. A large undeveloped wooded area began where Elmont Avenue ended. There was a pond, fed by a spring, a stone fireplace and an outhouse. My friends gigged for frogs but I never did. I never liked killing anything larger than a bug. I ice skated and played ice hockey when the pond froze over. The wooded area was a great spot for playing cowboys, army, building a tree house or just wandering around exploring. It also provided a short cut to some of my friends' homes. Imagine letting a child walk home in the dark through a woods today.

Lillian Holt donated a portion of this property to the county for a park and museum. Leslie and I visited there in 2008. The area around the pond is now clear of all the brush and many of the trees and is much more open. Picnic tables and benches are nearby. It is very well kept and incredibly neat. However, everything, including the pond, seems much smaller than I remember. It is unlike the wilderness that I remember that made it such a fun place to play.

Although we heated with oil, several house still heated with coal. The Hanna's, who lived across the street, burned soft coal because it was cheaper than hard coal. Periodically an accumulation of soot in the chimney caught fire. A fire truck came and put out the fire. As far as I know, there was never any damage.

A few people still used iceboxes but we always had a refrigerator.

MEMOIRS AND MORE

Home freezers and frozen foods were unknown. The refrigerator made ice cubes but had no space to freeze food. To get ice cubes out of the trays we ran water over the tray to loosen them. Mr. Oberender, whose son Alvin was a friend of mine, delivered ice to the few who still using iceboxes. On a hot day, we looked forward to him giving us chunks of ice. Once everyone owned a refrigerator, he started a moving van business. Mr. Oberender moved us twice. In 1957, he moved us from our apartment to our first house (Hilltop Avenue). Then in 1968, he moved us from Hilltop Avenue to Hamiltowne Circle.

Trash and garbage pickup was twice a week. There were no plastic garbage bags or plastic can liners at that time. An open truck picked up the garbage. A worker on the ground lifted the can to another on the truck who dumped the loose garbage at his feet. Before long, the man on the truck was knee deep in garbage. What was it like for him at the end of a hot summer day?

There was home delivery of several things. Mail came twice a day. Letters cost three cents and post cards cost one cent. Cloverland Dairy, their radio jingle was, "If you don't own a cow, call Cloverland now at North 9-2222," delivered the milk. This was very convenient and continued for a number of years after we moved to Rosedale. We put the money and a note listing what we wanted in an empty bottle and left it on the porch. The milk came in glass bottles with a cardboard top. In very cold weather, the milk froze and pushed the cardboard top up an inch or two above the top of the bottle. Capital Bakery delivered bread and other baked goods. Arabbers (long A) sold fruits and vegetables from horse drawn carts. Later a man I only knew as John, sold vegetables and eggs to us from a station wagon on both Hilltop Avenue and Hamiltowne Circle. During the soft crab season (the months with "r" in them), an old man (he seemed old to me) sold soft crabs. I can picture him walking up Elmont Avenue carrying a basket of soft crabs on each arm and calling out, "Soft crabs, soft crabs alive, soft crabs." A woman regularly came to Elmont Avenue selling inexpensive sewing items such as thread, pins, needles, etc. A Fuller

Brush man came every month selling a variety of sundry items.

Play, when I was a kid, was without parental intervention except for, "It's a nice day, go find somebody to play with." Kids rarely used the telephone to contact a friend. Typically, I would walk or bike to a friend's house, stand in front and call the person's name. We had a telephone but not the dial type. To make a call I told the operator the number and she (all telephone operators were female) connected you. We had a "party line" because it was less expensive. Several families had the same number but only one could use the telephone at a time. Our number was Boulevard 266R. My Aunt Thelma and Uncle Louis had Boulevard 266W. When another party was on their telephone, you could overhear the conversation.

Most play took place outside. There was a lot of playing with footballs, baseballs, basketballs, etc. but there were no real games. I had a scooter, a bicycle, and roller skates. We also played tag and various versions of step ball. Hide and seek, kick the can, capture the flag or redline could be played after dark. Card games and board games such as Monopoly were a last resort and usually played during bad weather.

My bicycle provided transportation to school, a store, a friend's house or to run errands. It was also an activity by itself. The bicycle club at Fullerton School planned group bike rides on Saturdays. My friends and I would ride to Middle River during World War II hoping to see them test fly a B-26. We biked to Memorial Stadium on 33rd Street to watch the construction. We made tandem bikes by removing the front wheel of one bike and putting the fork over the rear axle of another. This worked quite well. We wrapped a length of clothesline rope around the rear tire to see if that would work in snow like automobile tire chains. It didn't. We looked forward to snow, hoping it would close the schools. It was maddening when the school busses did not run because of snow but schools remained open. Those who rode the bus were off and I had to walk to school. Streets were not salted or plowed bare, therefore the snow stayed on streets longer.

After a few cars packed down the snow, sleigh riding could begin. If a plow came, we would line up across the street with our sleds upright in front of us blocking the street. Some days the driver would be sympathetic and just throw some ashes at the bottom of the hill. This would allow cars to get a start up the hill and let us continue sleigh riding longer.

As I grew a little older, I played baseball, football, soccer and basketball but nothing organized. A family on McCormick Avenue had an unused tennis court they let us fix up and use. There was no adult supervision. Rarely was there a real ball field and a limited amount of equipment was usually shared. It was unusual to have enough players for full teams so the rules changed based on the number of players present. Others joined the game as they showed up. The players umpired or referred their own games. We had to decide who would be on each team and who would play each position. We learned how to get along with others because we had to or there would be no game. We played for fun and we had fun. The fun lasted until adults organized and began to run the games for the children. This is a real loss for the current young people.

By necessity, but without being aware of it, we all learned valuable social lessons from these experiences. There were no coaches/managers directing teams or umpires/referees ruling on plays. Every decision was by consensus. There were differences, but arguments did not last long. Players yelled, "Was not" and "Was too" back and forth a few times then one would back down and the game continued. Although we were learning to negotiate, we did not know it.

Baseball often began when a few boys met at a field and played catch, or one would hit fly balls to the others in a game called "three flies in." The first person to catch three fly balls became the batter. An actual game would start well before there were enough for teams. A base would be a piece of cardboard or a rock. Nobody had a baseball uniform. We shared bats and gloves because not everyone had one. The catcher had no equipment other than his glove. When I left my position in the field to bat, I left my glove there fore my replacement. Foul lines and the number of bases depended upon the number of players. There were no coaches so the players umpired the game. In a game called "rotation," two, three or four players would be batters and the remainder the fielders. The batters remained batters until they made an out. If the batter hit a fly ball that was caught the batter and the fielder switched places. If the batter was out any other way, he went to left field and everyone else moved up a notch, the pitcher becoming a batter, etc. If there were an adequate number we would play a "choose up" game. Two boys alternated selecting players for his team, the better players always chosen first. I was good enough not to embarrass myself but never chosen early. Others joined as they arrived. Everyone played who wanted to. The process was similar for all the other sports.

We played "mob" soccer every morning at Fullerton School. This is one instance where there were always more than enough people for teams. Whoever got to school first would get a soccer ball from the school custodian. A game began as soon as there were six or eight boys there. As others arrived, they arbitrarily decided which team to play on. Eventually thirty to forty boys would be playing. Nobody kept score. The game was over when the bell rang for the start of classes.

We formed a neighborhood baseball team. There was no league and I'm not certain we ever played a game except among ourselves. Woody Woodhall, about twenty years old, was our manager. We decided to make a baseball diamond. The Gardens of Faith cemetery is there now but nothing was there at that time. In fact, for several years I cut our Christmas tree from there. Actually, I cut two each time. It was impossible to find a well-shaped tree. After I got home, I cut branches off the second tree to fill in the bare spots in the first. One afternoon Woody decided we should burn the weeds to clear the ground for the infield. The fire got a little out of hand. We beat it out. At least, we thought we had. That night it flared up again and the fire department came and put it out. I was scared that the police or fire department would be after us, but nothing happened. We were fortunate that there were no houses nearby. On the bright side, the second fire finished clearing the infield for us. It also cleared much of the outfield as well.

Saturday was movie day At the Overlea Theater. I always picked the aisle seat in the last row on the right side. For thirteen cents, I saw a feature film, short subject, cartoon, news and a serial. The serial always ended with the hero in a seemingly impossible situation. This would entice me to come back the following week. I could go in at any time during the movie and stay as long as I wanted.

The Overlea Theater hired teenagers as ushers, more to keep order than seat people. Mason Clift was both a friend and an usher. Occasionally I would get a free pass from him. Now and then, he let me sneak in through an exit door. Why either one of us would take a chance on being caught for thirteen cents makes no sense at all. I guess it was the element of danger. If caught, there would be no way this could be justified to my mother and father. The Paramount Theater, more modern, opened three blocks away next to the Overlea Diner. I continued to go to the Overlea Theater because the Paramount charged eighteen cents.

The closest thing I had to a brother or sister was a foster child type of person who lived with us for a while. I had not thought about Edith Islaub in many years until I began writing this. From my note to Santa Claus in 1940 in my mother's scrapbook, I know she was living with us then. It is a mystery to me how, when or why she came or exactly when she left. I remember that she helped me with my homework. She was older than I was and had a boy friend in the navy named Bud. The three of us played the card game war. Her mother lived on a farm. After a visit there she brought back a live chicken which she killed by snapping its neck. After Edith graduated from Kenwood High School she and Bud married.

My grandmother's sister, Aunt Leona, owned a shore home on a creek somewhere in Middle River. Family members frequently came to visit. Sometimes they just came for the day, other times they stayed for a weekend or even longer. I don't know how many bedrooms there were but if a large group stayed overnight, everyone slept in the same large room. A curtain divided the room in two. The men slept on one side of the curtain, and women on the other. The telephone had a hand crank used to reach the operator in order to make a call. The phone was on a party line. Each family's telephone had its own distinct ring. When a call came in, every phone on the party line rang. To tell if the call was for you it was necessary to listen to the number of short and long rings.

Everyone rowed across the creek to swim where there was a sandy beach. It was very shallow and very safe. One day my mother rowed me across to play in the water. I hid behind the boat and kept very quiet. I thought I was being funny, but I scared the life out of her.

One morning I got up early and fished from the shore. I managed to hook a sunfish. Not wanting to touch the fish to get it off the hook, I woke my father to do it for me. In the winter, the creek would freeze over now and then. My grandfather would push a rowboat into the middle of the creek and sit in it to fish through the ice.

Ron Mueller, my cousin, spent a week there with my family and me. We were there on a Sunday because I remember my parents driving the two of us to Epiphany Lutheran Church in Overlea so Ron could maintain his perfect attendance record at Sunday school. I often went to there with him but perfect attendance at Sunday school was not one of my priorities.

Benny Schott lived nearby and came around for handouts. I do not know if he had family there or not. He rarely washed, usually needed a shave and frequently smelled bad. Once I watched as my father and Uncle George dragged Benny into the river and made him wash. Apparently, making Benny take a bath in the river was a regular occurrence whenever my father and uncle were there. He appears very happy in a picture I have him. Is the smile because he just had a bath or avoided one?

Most often when my parents took me swimming it was to a public beach. Usually it was Rocky Point Park or Porters. Once, when I was about six, we rented a cabin at New Fairview Beach with my Aunt Jean and Uncle George. There was electricity for light but instead of a refrigerator, there was an icebox. A truck delivered ice every day or two. There was a square sign with the numbers 25, 50, 75 or 100 that we placed in the kitchen window to tell the iceman how much ice to leave. The beach where we swam was just a few steps from our front door. Ft. Smallwood Park was nearby. We went to crab and fish from the pier at Ft. Smallwood. For a treat, we drove to Riveria Beach for ice cream. The place we went to manufactured the ice cream. I could watch as they made various flavors.

Now and then, my father took me fishing. First, we rented a rowboat at Steven's Marina. Then we would row out and start fishing next to a nearby duck blind. That is where the white and yellow perch were supposed to be. Sometimes they were there sometimes they were not. If we were not catching fish in one spot, we would row to another. Neither of us talked much. Actually, we probably never talked at all. How many fish we caught was not important, I just liked being there with him. Besides, except for canned tuna, I never ate fish then and do not eat it now.

In the spring and again in the fall it was time for house cleaning. These were annual events for almost every family. In addition to cleaning there were modifications related to the change in seasons. To prepare for cold weather, we hung light colored shades at the windows to let the sun in. Wool carpets covered the floors for warmth. At open doorways, heavy drapes called portieres, hung in open stopped drafts. My mother and I did these jobs together. We did not work well together, but we laughed a lot. My grandfather made storm windows for the entire house. These were heavy and hung on the outside of each window to keep heat in and cold out. It was possible to change the first floor storm windows from the outside using a stepladder. The second floor was a different story. (No pun intended.) You had to work from inside the house while holding a heavy storm window outside and try to hang it on two brackets at the top of the frame that you could not see. I remember doing those on the first floor but not on the second. The reverse happened in the spring. Dark blue shades replaced the light colored shades, jute summer rugs replaced the wool rugs. Down came the portieres and the storm windows. Awnings replaced the storm windows to keep the out the heat of the sun.

The Brown's, friends of my parents, raised corn on the farm they owned. We visited them regularly. Mr. Brown asked if I would like to go hunting for the groundhogs that were destroying his corn crop. Thinking, or perhaps not thinking at all, it might be fun, I said, "yes." He handed me a twenty-two rifle and off we went. About ten minutes later, I spotted one, took aim and fired. The groundhog yelped once, leaped straight up and then flopped to the ground. Mr. Brown told me it was a great shot, especially since this was my first time hunting. It was also my last. I never went hunting again. I still feel sorry for the groundhog. You would think I would have learned something from that experience. If I had, I would never have started my rabbit business.

Gail Thomas, who lived across the street, gave me her male pet rabbit named Bimbis. Another friend, Chris Wild, raised and sold rabbits. In another, "It seemed like a good idea at the time," decision, I got a female rabbit from Chris and began my business. My grandfather built the cages for the rabbits. I had no trouble raising them. When I had about twenty-five, it was time to begin to reap some profit. Only then did I think about how I was going to accomplish this. What was I thinking? Chris told me all I had to do was hold them by the ears, whack them in the back of the neck with a piece of pipe and skin them. I did not mind them being dead but there was no way I was going to be the one to do it. A friend of my parents, Chauncey Showalter, killed and skinned all of them except Bimbis. I am glad I was not there to see it. We kept a few to eat and gave Chauncey the remainder. I was out of the rabbit business. Bimbis went to the Brown's farm where either he lived to a ripe old age or the Browns got hungry, whichever came first.

It is only looking back that I can see how lucky I was to live with my grandparents. They took me to Linden Farm to visit Fred (my grandfather's brother?) and Anna Dannenfelser. Although I called them Aunt and Uncle, I am not sure of the actual relationship.

The following information is from an article about Linden Farm in the Saturday, March 26, 1932 issue of, *"The Jeffersonian."* The property comprised a thousand acres bisected by Belair Road just north of Joppa Road owned by George Calvert Lord Baltimore. The property was surveyed in September of 1683 for a John Darnell who came to Maryland with Lord Baltimore. Around 1832, a Philip Dannenfelser, Sr. acquired approximately two hundred twenty acres of the property. He divided the property among his children at his death. The house and seventy acres went to his son, a Frederick Dannenfelser. (The exact relationship of Philip, Sr. and Frederic to my grandfather is not clear. My grandfather was Philip Jr. but it unlikely his father would have owned property in 1832. Perhaps my grandfather was Phillip Dannenfelser, III.)

There was no electricity or central heat. A wood/coal burning kitchen stove and a fireplace provided the heat. The drinking water came from a spring. Light came from kerosene lanterns. I suppose there was an icebox but I do not remember one. I saw some food as it cooled in a "spring house" chilled by water from a nearby spring. Linden Farm provided both the cedar trees and stones for the rock garden on Elmont Avenue. A piece of a tree limb growing around a horseshoe found on Linden Farm is now a doorstop in our apartment.

THE GREATEST GRANDPARENTS

Eleanor and Philip Dannenfelser were the perfect grandparents. Many Saturdays, I went with them to shop and to get something to eat at the Monument Street Market. I remember getting oyster stew that came with little round oyster crackers. Sometimes we would also see a movie and vaudeville show at the State Theater nearby. It was important to get to the movie on time. If we were late and missed the first part of the movie, we never stayed to see the beginning. My grandparents took me to the New York Worlds Fair. It was a last minute idea. We left before my parents realized we were gone. A telegram sent from the World's Fair from me to my mother indicates I was at the fair on July 13, 1941. This may have been how they learned where we were. I recall three things about the fair. First, there was a demonstration of television. It was another five or six years before TV became commercially available. Second, Esther Williams, a swimmer and later a movie star, performed. I can still picture her poised on a diving board. Finally, there were about six or eight swimmers in a large pool who demonstrated synchronized swimming.

When I was young, every circus performed in tents rather than in arenas. My grandparents took me to one that I believe was set up at Monument Street and Pulaski Highway. There may have been a large tent or "big top" with the typical animals, clowns, acrobats, etc. All I remember are the "side shows." Barkers, I think that is what they called them, stood outside these smaller tents attempting to lure people in. There were sword swallowers, fire-eaters, snake handlers, overly fat people, exceedingly thin people, outlandishly tattooed people, bearded women, etc. Any deformed person or freak of nature that people would pay to look at could be on display. These acts are "politically incorrect" today.

When my grandparents knew Lois and I were serious, they treated her as they would a granddaughter. One summer before we married they took us to Atlantic City. Coming home, I began to wonder why my legs bothered me so much. We stopped to eat and I saw my legs were sunburned beet red. We were not on the beach very long that day, but apparently the combination of water, sand and salt air magnified the sun's effect. I was sore for days.

My mother remembers her father as a very strict disciplinarian. I know him to be anything but that. He was a neat grandfather. Once, when I wondered what the basement looked like from the first floor, he drilled a hole in the rear of a closet so I could peek through. He did a lot of carpentry work in the basement. Other kids had toy tool sets. He gave me the real things along with scrap wood and nails and I would hammer and saw along with him. I drove so many nails in the cellar steps he had to replace many of them. Why would he allow me to do that? It could only be love.

I kept my pedal car in a little garage that my grandfather built for me. He included a gas pump so that I never had to worry about running out of gas. During a WW II, my contribution to a scrap metal drive was this little car. I recently read that at that time gas was about nineteen cents a gallon and a new car could be purchased for a thousand dollars or less.

Every year my grandfather, I thought it was Santa Claus, built a large Christmas garden in the basement. He began on Thanksgiving and worked every day until late Christmas Eve. I could not see anything until Christmas morning so my anticipation increased each day. With the basement door locked and the windows covered, I could not even peek. Once I no longer believed in Santa Claus, we built the garden together. He purchased some of the items in the garden, but preferred to make them by adapting something he had at hand. He was

MARVIN LEROY OED

very inventive. The bars for the cages of a zoo he built were straws painted black. He made a sheet metal swimming pool that fit into a hole in the platform and filled with water. The swimmers in the pool were naked plastic baby dolls held up in the water by a stand. He painted bathing suits on them. Lead soldiers and other people were popular at that time. He made a golfer into a boy flying a kite by attaching one end of a stiff wire to the golf club and the other to a piece of paper shaped as a kite. The roads were actual concrete, mixed and poured into forms. The grass was sawdust he dyed green. The vegetable garden had real dirt. Bushes and trees were fashioned from bits of real evergreen trees. All the buildings lit up. The electric wires were under the platform that was about three feet above the floor. Wiring was in series then. Therefore, if one bulb burned out every light went out. My job was to crawl underneath with what resembled a pair of pliers with insulated handles and pointed teeth. Lying on my back, I would work my way from one bulb to the next squeezing the two wires coming from the bulb with the pliers. When the pliers completed the circuit at the defective bulb, the others would come back on. Then I knew which bulb to replace. This was the same method used for Christmas tree lights until parallel light strings became available.

There was craftiness about his sense of humor. When I was little he kept me guessing what one Christmas present was going to be by saying, "it has two up, four down and one out each end" while demonstrating by pointing his fingers and thumbs. Christmas morning I learned these were the ears, legs, nose and tail of the fox terrier puppy that was my present. I named my puppy Patsy because that was the name of the dog owned my Mr. and Mrs. Wolfe who lived across the street. I cannot explain why. I was very upset when a milk truck killed Patsy. My grandfather replaced Patsy with another fox terrier almost immediately. Not very creative, I named him Spot. Another year he gave me a piece of flat metal about two inches by eight inches. He said it was a part of my Christmas present and I should shine it. Every day or two he handed me another one. I knew from the expression on his face that he was having fun with me. I dutifully polished all ten of them without ever learning why. Christmas morning my surprise was the pool table he built for me. Embellishing the table were the metal strips I had spent so much time working on.

My grandfather often played catch with me and occasionally took me fishing. We fished from a rowboat and used bamboo poles and bobbers just like Opie in Mayberry. I was very young when he took me to the Timonium Fairground to see the animals. As far as I know, he never ever went to a horse race. Nevertheless, he bought tickets for the races that day. Now and then, he took me to International League Baltimore Oriole games. He liked to sit in the bleachers. There was a bowling alley beneath the Overlea Theater. When he first took me, I was so young that even though these were duckpins I had to use two hands to roll the ball down the alley.

We were in our house on Hilltop Avenue only a short time when I slipped while mowing the steep slope in the front. My foot went under the mower and I ended up in the emergency room at Sinai Hospital (located on Monument Street at that time). Fortunately the damage was minimal, a broken great toe and cuts across the bottoms of the other toes. By the time I got back from the hospital, my grandfather had finished mowing the slope. To keep from slipping he drove nails through the soles of a pair of old work shoes. They looked like golf shoes with three-inch long spikes. He couldn't slip even if he tried. As I said before, he was inventive.

Like many people, he reached the point where he could function at home but could not understand that he should no longer be driving. Not knowing what else to do, I asked to borrow his car. He readily agreed. I never returned it. Later, even when he was talking to me, he would say, "That boy took my car and never brought it back." His tone was not anger, just matter-of-fact. He never realized that I was "that boy" who took his car.

The earliest memory I have of my grandmother is her reading the comics to me at their kitchen table. For some reason the one that comes to mind is Uncle Wiggily Longears. The little things in life can be so important. I have a fond memory of sitting with my grandmother at her kitchen window on a snowy winter evening watching for my grandfather to come home from work. During summer storms, we would sit at the same window and watch the lightening flashes in the sky.

While growing up, I wanted to mow the lawn, but I only had the strength to push the reel type mower where the grass was sparse. Then we got a power mower that had reel type cutters but connected to a motor that turned the reel. Now I was able to mow the entire lawn. My grandmother was impatient when it came to getting things done and always wanted to help. I would barely start mowing when my grandmother would get out the old reel mower to help me. It was embarrassing. I certainly did not want anyone to see my grandmother using the hand mower while I used the power mower. Somehow, this dilemma was eventually resolved and I mowed the entire lawn.

WORLD WAR II (1941-1945)

WW II changed life in the United States and much of the world. Following World War I until December 7, 1941, there was a countrywide isolationist sentiment and resistance to a military draft. Following the Japanese attack on Pearl Harbor and Germany declaring war on the United States, the country became unified in an all out war effort. This was arguably the last war to have the full support of the people of the United States. The United Service Organization (USO) provided entertainment and other services for those in the military. My parents were helping at one of their affairs and I went along. There was food, dancing and entertainment provided free for anyone in the armed services. People were proud to have family members in the military. Red, white and blue banners hung in a window identified those with a family member in the service. Most had a blue star in the center. A gold star replacing the blue one indicated the soldier died.

Patriotism was very high. In addition to those drafted, volunteers began filling the ranks of the military. High schools graduated students early so they could enlist in the services. Entire athletic teams enlisted as a group. War Bonds, now called savings bonds, helped finance that war. Schools sold savings stamps for twenty-five cents each. Every week I bought several and pasted them in a book. I filled my book with seventy-five stamps ($18.75) then exchanged it for a bond that would be worth $25.00 in ten years. I filled out the form with my father's name and received the bond. I thought my father's name was Bernard until I showed the bond to my mother. It was then I learned his real name was Benjamin and had to have the bond corrected. I never heard anyone call him Benjamin. All his friends called him Bernie or Bernard. Everyone knew him as "Ben" at work. I learned that when I telephone there, no one knew who Bernard was.

Grocery stores collected used cooking fats. I seem to remember the fat having something to do with the manufacture of explosives. Periodically there were drives to collect scrap metal. I took my pedal car out to the gutter, no curbs yet, for one of these drives.

Gasoline, tires, cars, fuel oil, meat, sugar, coffee, silk, nylon, and shoes were scarce and rationed. Everyone received a limited number of the stamps or tokens needed to purchase scarce items. Heating oil was frequently in short supply. Sometimes we ran out of oil for a few days. The main source of heat then was our kitchen stove.

Periodically, there were air raid drills at night. Everything stopped when the air raid siren sounded. No house lights could be visible from outside. My grandfather was a volunteer air raid warden. When an alert sounded, his job was to walk the neighborhood to make certain everyone complied with the lights out rule. We qualified for an extension telephone in our basement since he was an air raid warden. Why was there a need for a telephone in the basement?

My father left his job as a paper cutter to work at the Glenn L. Martin Company in Middle River. Martin built PBY seaplanes and B-26 bombers. My mother worked at Martin's also, but in an office. The buildings and large number of cars on the parking lots would be a dead give away to enemy pilots. The buildings were painted to camouflage them and the parking lots were covered with a mesh to make them look like an open field from the air. Likewise, open land nearby was made to appear to be a residential neighborhood by laying out streets and lining them with mock homes similar to those used to film movies. However, these had only a roof whereas the movie houses had only a front. The thousands of workers coming into the Baltimore area during the war needed housing. The communities of Aero Acres and Victory Villa were built to help meet that need. The Sadlers, our neighbors at the corner of Kenwood Avenue, rented one large room to several men. Men working different shifts shared a bed.

My grandfather left his job at Gamse Lithographing to build liberty ships at Bethlehem-Fairfield Shipyard. My grandmother, grandfather and I went to watch a ship launched. Only two of the almost three thousand built during WW II remain. The John W. Brown, built at the Bethlehem-Fairfield Shipyard, is now a floating/cruising museum berthed at Locust Point Marine Terminal. Built in just fifty-four days, an amazing effort, the John Brown ferried troops and POW's as well as cargo, and participated in the invasion of France in 1944.

There were many unsung heroes during WW II. Those sailing the liberty ships are among the least recognized. Armed Guard units provided by the Navy operated the guns, but it was merchant marines, all civilian volunteers, who knowingly sailed the extremely dangerous seas. They began ferrying supplies to our future allies before the United Stated became involved, and were the first U.S. casualties of the war. German submarines sank a number of them within sight of the Atlantic and Gulf coasts of the United States. Sadly, many merchant marines lost their lives early in the war because large cities on these coastlines remained well lighted for economic reasons. This silhouetted the ships and made them easy targets for the U-Boats' torpedoes.

In 1945, President Roosevelt died and Harry Truman became president of the United States. There was a great deal of doubt about his capabilities because he was a virtual unknown. The following year Truman authorized the dropping of the atomic bombs on Hiroshima and Nagasaki that ended World War II. The development of an atomic bomb was a secret in the United States and the rest of the world. The attack on Hiroshima was as much of a surprise to the American people as it was to the Japanese. Even Truman did not learn of the atomic bomb until after becoming president. The estimate was there would be one million allied losses if there were a land invasion of Japan. Hence, there was little discussion at the time whether the attacks were justifiable or not. The debate whether the bombings, particularly of

Nagasaki, avoided an invasion and saved up to a million allied lives or unnecessarily killed hundreds of thousands of innocent Japanese began sometime later. Truman became one of my favorite presidents because he was forthright and down to earth. He could also display some fatherly emotion. Paul Humes, a Washington Post reporter, criticized the singing of Truman's daughter Margaret. Truman responded with a letter that concluded, "Some day I hope to meet you. When that happens you'll need a new nose, a lot of beefsteak for black eyes and perhaps a supporter below."

I was almost eleven years old when my father came home early from work August 15, 1945, the day President Truman announced Japan's surrender. He arrived sitting on the top of the back seat of a convertible with a car full of men laughing, yelling and waving. Later that evening we went downtown. I remember being at the corner of Pratt and Light Streets. There were so many people there celebrating the end of the war that it was like Times Square in New York City on New Years Eve. I cannot imagine how we drove downtown or found a place to park. No streetcar went by without someone pulling the trolley off the wire and stopping it, sometimes multiple times. Nobody cared. A terrible war was over. I imagine this was as much a sign of relief as it was a celebration.

EDUCATION—SCHOOL ENDURED, NOT ENJOYED

There was no kindergarten in Baltimore County at that time so I began school in the first grade at Fullerton Elementary/Junior High School. Elmont Avenue is about a half mile away so we all walked to school. The short cut was across a large open field at Kenwood Avenue. Now and then, the owner, old Mrs. Marx, would chase us waving a broom. We were never sure why. Once across her property, it was a short walk through some woods and across Linden and Beech Avenues to the school. The few black people in Overlea lived on these two blocks, known as Cherry Heights.

I tolerated, rather than liked, school. I looked forward to the things that got me out of class such as recess, fire drills, air raid drills, (this was WW II), assemblies, lunch, snow days, etc. Gym class was OK but summer vacation was the best. What word can I use to describe my academic performance at Fullerton Elementary? Unremarkable is good because it is adequately vague. Not intentionally, but unwisely, I developed an approach to education that stayed with me even into college. I knew it was necessary to go to school, but I never took education seriously. In order to make the best of it, I was seldom a discipline problem. In elementary school, a Mrs. Huntington, substituting for our regular teacher, assigned a writing project. I raised my hand and asked her how to spell "chrysanthemum." She knew my intent was to embarrass her, and led to a trip to the principles office and a note to my parents. When my mother read the letter, I learned that the Huntington's were their friends. She was embarrassed. I did not usually bother my teachers and hoped they would not bother me. This was wrong time to be a smart-aleck. I never took education seriously. I did what I had to do to pass the tests and move on to the next grade. Excelling was never my center of attention. I never related education to having any future value.

When my parents had a large party, they hired a woman from Cherry Heights to help clean up and wash dishes. This was just a stones throw from Fullerton School. Black kids lived in Cherry Heights, but none attended Fullerton School even though it was just a block away. To this day I have no idea where, or even if, they went to school. There was a makeshift board fence across Linden and Beech Avenues to prevent traffic from going from the black to white sections of these streets. At that time, blacks and whites did not live in the same neighborhoods, go to the same schools, socialize, play, eat in the same restaurants, go to the same movies, or swim at the same beaches. As I look back, I find it curious that I never thought of this as unusual or wrong. This was racial prejudice but I never gave it any thought. That is just the way it was at that time.

Prejudices applied to other groups, particularly Jews, as well. I knew the "Restricted" sign at Miami Beach Park in Bowley's Quarters and other beaches meant blacks and Jews could not swim there. I remember coming back from Atlantic City with my grandparents and seeing a "No Blacks Allowed," (it more likely said colored or negroes) sign at the entrance to a restaurant. Because, "that's the way it was," I just wondered where they ate, not whether it was right or wrong. To a lesser extent, there were prejudices toward other ethnic and religious groups. There was generally disapproval of marriage between Christians and Jews and Protestants and Catholics. While they may have worked together, lived in the same neighborhood and respected each other, most parents were less than thrilled if their child married into another ethnic or religious group.

Nobody ever drove there kids to school. I detested using the umbrella that my mother made me take. It is not my nature to argue when there is another way. The Sadlers' house at the corner of Kenwood Avenue had a very high hedge. I hid the umbrella in the hedge on the way to school and picked it up on the way home. I do the same thing now on my way to exercise at the gym. Lois will tell me that I need a jacket when I do not think it is that cold outside. I put it on anyway. When I get to the parking lot, I put the jacket in the car, walk to the gym and then pick it up on the way back. That keeps us both happy.

I thought of my mother as quiet. That may be true except for her card club. In warm weather, all the windows in the house were open. Coming home from school, I could tell when it was card club day. Eight people playing cards were all talking at the same time. It was loud enough that I heard them before I crossed Kenwood Avenue.

At Fullerton most of my elementary school report cards included a comment such as, "Marvin is not working up to his potential." I never saw any reason to. I passed with little or no effort, albeit with lackluster, good enough for me, grades. Each quarter my mother signed the report card and I returned it to school. My solution, when one quarter's report card was more lackluster than usual, was to alter one or two of the grades before my mother signed it and then changed them back before turning it in to the school. My Fullerton Junior High School performance was equally as unremarkable as elementary school. My memory of the educational aspect of these years is limited. It could have not have been good because my mother had to make several, she would tell you many, trips to meet with one teacher or another.

Mrs. Cohen taught Core, a combination of several courses in the eighth grade. Poor Mrs. Cohen, for some reason the class singled her out to torment. One person would begin tapping his desk with a pencil. Gradually everyone else would join in. Other times one person would begin humming quietly and eventually there would be a low hmmmmm from the entire class. This even occurred on parents' visiting day. By a stroke of bad luck for Mrs. Cohen, her class was the one chosen for the parents to visit. I tied one corner of a handkerchief to a button on my shirt, ran it inside a sleeve and out the cuff. We hummed and tapped pencils. I would pretend to blow my nose. When I straightened my arm anyone watching, my mother was, would see the handkerchief magically disappear up my sleeve. I do not remember any repercussions, recall Mrs. Cohen saying anything about our behavior or having the principal in to discipline us. We sure earned it. Even my mother had little to say to me about it. Maybe she did not because the entire class participated.

The last desks in Mrs. Cohen's classroom backed up to the windows. There was no air conditioning so the windows were open during warm weather. Occasionally, a book on the window ledge "accidentally" fell out. Going outside to retrieve the book provided a little diversion from the tedium of school.

Television was still a novelty in 1947 when we bought ours. According to what I read recently there were only about one million television sets in the entire United States at that time. There was no color TV, only black and white. The ten-inch screen, much smaller than today's, was standard. A magnifying glass was available to hang over the screen to provide a larger picture. We first used an indoor rabbit ears antenna. Later there was an antenna installed on the roof. The only stations we received were the three local channels (Channel 2 WMAR, Channel 11 WBAL, and Channel 13 WAAM). All three signed off with the Star Spangled Banner at about ten or eleven in the evening. There were no taped shows. All broadcasts were live. If someone misspoke, sometimes causing the entire cast and audience to break up in laughter, there was no way to delete it. Entire shows were made of the funniest of these "bloopers."

My seventh grade class periodically held parties at one of our parent's homes. Our television was the focus of attention at a party at my house because many in the class did not have a TV of there own at home. Charles and Naomi Zipp, relatives and close friends of my parents, came to visit regularly just to watch television.

There was an effort to suppress inappropriate language, dress, and anything deemed coarse or vulgar on TV. This lasted into the 1950's and perhaps beyond. In January of 1957, Lois and I saw Elvis Presley appear on Ed Sullivan's Sunday night variety show, "Toast of the Town." The cameras only showed him from the waist up. That way no one saw him swivel his hips. In another instance, a female singer was required to pin a handkerchief to her dress to cover some cleavage. This may have been an over reaction, but I believe it to be better than the opposite extremes of today.

Occasionally, we would walk from Fullerton School to the Overlea Bowling Alley for a gym class. There were no automatic pin setting machines at that time. The bowling alley hired pin boys to clear the dead wood, reset the pins and put the balls on a rail to return them to the bowler. To reset the pins exactly where they belonged there was a pedal below the alley. The pin boy stepped on the pedal and ten rods about an inch long came up in the alley where each pin was to go. The pins had a hole that fit over the rod. After the pins were in place, the pin boy took his foot away and the rods dropped back down. During gym class, boys from the class volunteered to become pin boys. I thought it was fun to be a pin boy. As I look back this was probably not a very good idea, especially for those like me with no experience. I had to be alert. Pins fly all over the place, even some from the adjacent alleys. Now and then, someone rolled a ball down the alley before I cleared the dead wood and got out of the way. Luck was the only reason no one was hurt.

While walking home from school we often met a boy, we, not unkindly, called "Crazy Joe." I never learned his real name. I now believe he suffered from Down's syndrome. Crazy Joe liked to watch boys fight and thought he knew how to dance. Two boys would stage a fight for him and then Joe would dance for us. He laughed and seemed to be having a good time. I like to think we brightened his day.

At that time, Kenwood High School was located on Philadelphia

Road in the building that is now Rosedale Middle School. My scholastic performance continued much like before. I never connected my education with my future and only did what I had to do to get by. On the positive side, I found I liked algebra, geometry and trigonometry and did well in these. Looking back, I think it was because they involved problem solving. I guess I felt there was some purpose to that.

Kenwood fielded baseball, basketball, track and soccer (football was not permitted) teams, and provided my first chance at organized sports. I tried out for baseball but did not make the team. There were too many players better than I was. Then I tried out for cross-country. I was never particularly fast, but I thought I might do okay over the longer (3 miles?) distance. Several weeks into practice, the team went to Clifton Park where we could simulate an actual cross county race. My tongue was dragging on the ground but I was keeping up with the group as we neared the finish line. Then the coach said, "Kick it up and sprint to the finish." Kick it up and sprint to the finish! I would be lucky if I could crawl at the finish. I ended my track career that day.

The Drama Club wanted boys to volunteer to dance the can-can for a variety program. Mason Clift, a friend, raised his hand to volunteer and then I did. I cannot imagine why. It must have been a friendship reflex. I was too shy for anything like this. I never volunteered for anything in twelve years of school. However, this! What was I thinking? Caught up in the moment I guess. However, I was never one to back out of something. There was no way out. I had to go through with it.

We rented the costumes, high heels and all. None of us could even stand in the shoes much less dance. We switched to high top tennis shoes. Only girls wore low cut sneakers then. What a sight we were! Try to picture twelve high school boys with hairy legs wearing lipstick and high top tennis shoes attempting to dance. We were not the Rockettes.

Unknown to the teacher who taught us the dance routine we decided to spice up our act at the end by running off the stage into the audience and kissing our male math teacher. We liked him and thought he would be a good sport. He was. That night he left with a face full of lipstick.

We looked so bad, danced so bad and were so out-and-out awful that we were the hit of the show. Lois was there. In spite of this performance, we continued to date.

For the coming senior year, I signed up only for the required courses. After all, that was all I needed to meet the state's graduation requirements. Why do more? This left a large number, about a dozen as I recall, of study periods. The guidance counselor said she did not care how few credits I needed, I was not going to have all those study periods. I selected what I felt were the easiest courses available. First, I selected Typing for Personal Use. It had to be easier than Business Typing. Second, I chose Mechanical Drawing I. That should not be too demanding. I had a little mechanical drawing as part of the shop course at Fullerton that would give me a leg up. Knowing how to type turned out to be very useful in pharmacy school and throughout my career in pharmacy. Knowing how to touch type made writing this much easier. I really liked mechanical drawing and later on even considered applying for a job as a draftsman. Although chosen for the wrong reason both courses turned out to be good choices. I made good use of both skills.

At last, my final year of high school arrived. I would graduate in June 1952. I had no idea what I would do after that, but I didn't care. The only thing I wanted was to get out of Kenwood High School. Since I could pass the tests with little effort there was little reason to do any homework. One teacher saw it differently. I failed to turn in several homework assignments. She then contacted the guidance counselor and said I would fail the course (required for graduation) unless I satisfactorily completed all of the homework. The guidance counselor telephoned my mother. My mother was distraught when the counselor told her, "Marvin's graduation from Kenwood is unlikely, and, if he should graduate, he will not be accepted into college. If he should be accepted into a college, he certainly wouldn't graduate." This is not news a mother wants to hear. I assumed it was just a scare tactic. Thinking back while writing this, I undoubtedly caused my mother and father more anguish than I thought at the time. I was called to the guidance office and told to complete all the incomplete homework assignments and all the assignments, or else. I made up the work and graduated on time.

See, I was right. Why worry.

I NEED A COLLEGE AND A CAREER

I was in my senior year and still had no idea what I wanted to do after graduation. As usual, my parents were more concerned than I was because I was never concerned about anything related to my education. As I think about it, I must be an optimist because I am not sure that I was ever concerned about anything. However, my parents let me know that I would go to college. We were at the Copper Kettle restaurant on Belair Road having our customary Sunday lunch before a movie when the topic of my career came up. My father mentioned that a friend of his owned Belmar Pharmacy and had retired at age fifty. There was hardly any discussion. We were three very quiet people. Discussions were rare. Actually, it is possible that we had never really discussed anything. Early retirement provided as good a reason as any for choosing a career. In another, "It seemed like a good idea at the time," decision, I applied to the University of Maryland School of Pharmacy the following week. At least I made a choice and could forget about it. This was not the ideal way to choose a career, but it actually turned out very well for me.

It will come as no surprise to anyone who has read this far, that my high school transcripts were not exemplary. During the summer of 1952, a letter arrived. The University of Maryland at Baltimore School of Pharmacy accepted me for the fall semester. Either I did very well on the entrance exam or the pharmacy school was desperate because it certainly was not my grade point average. What would I have done had they not accepted me? I don't know what I would have done made had no other option. Acceptance, despite my misguided approach to education, only reinforced an already poor mind-set. That attitude continued into the first semester at pharmacy school. I never attached any importance to any course or topic that I felt was unrelated to being a pharmacist. An introductory pharmacy course made sense. However, when would I ever have to speak German, need to know the Bessemer steel process or solve quadratic equations in order to fill a prescription? Before the end of the semester, I knew my grades were not going to be good. The last day, not even waiting to see my grades, I decided I would quit pharmacy school. Instead of going home, I went to the Glenn L. Martin Company. I hoped my one year of mechanical drawing in high school would qualify me for an entry-level job. The employment office closed before I got there. Although not immediately appreciated, this was a stroke of luck for me. By the time the second semester began, I had been convinced to go back to school.

Because of my low grade point average the first semester, I was unable to continue pledging Phi Delta Chi fraternity and repeated one course the following summer. I caught up and began my second year on schedule. I liked the courses that included laboratory sessions that had measurable outcomes. In pharmacology, I could actually demonstrate a drug's effect on an animal. Using qualitative analysis, I determined if a particular drug was present. In quantitative analysis, I measured exactly how much of a particular drug was present. I may not have liked courses that I considered irrelevant, but I had learned that this was not high school and I could no longer just show up and get by.

I graduated on time with a reasonable GPA, but without any fondness for the School of Pharmacy. I did what I had to do in order to become a pharmacist and was just glad to get out. Even graduation held little importance to me. I went, mainly for my parents. I skipped the parties that followed the ceremony and worked the evening shift at a Reads Drug Store.

My attitude regarding education changed dramatically once I graduated from pharmacy school. I began taking courses I thought would be useful. Once I found that I could determine what I would learn about, I thoroughly enjoyed it. What a transformation. I took business and computer courses at Essex Community College and the University of Maryland Baltimore County. Spectro Industries provided an educational program that prepared me for the medical equipment and orthotics business. In preparation for adding respiratory care to our medical equipment service, Tedd Pruss arranged for me to spend time with an anesthesiologist at the University of Pennsylvania Hospital. Various manufacturers provided seminars related to the items we were providing. My curriculum vitae while I was teaching at the School of Pharmacy listed thirty-one courses and seminars under Non-Degree programs. I estimate that I participated in at least fifty hours of business related seminars provided by Medicine Shoppe International. As much as I disliked my formal education, I loved learning this way.

One business seminar I participated in included a segment on setting goals. It a community pharmacist set any goals at all it was usually to increase sales, the number of prescriptions dispensed or gross profit. This seminar taught that these are merely hopes and too vague to be useful. An effective goal must be written, define a specific task and be measurable. This was a polished version of my to-do list concept.

UNCLE SAM WANTS ME

I was exempt from the military draft until I graduated from Pharmacy School. I expected to be called up shortly after I graduated. It seemed to me that having some prior National Guard experience could be helpful. In 1953, I enlisted in Headquarters Company, Maryland National Guard, 29th Infantry Division, G-2 Section. We met weekly downtown at the Richmond Market and Fifth Regiment Armories, and spent two weeks at summer camp each year.

I missed something along the way because I was rarely sure what it was that I was doing or supposed to be doing. This seems incongruous, especially for an intelligence section. Nobody seemed to care, so I did not. At least, in uniform, I think I looked the part of a soldier.

Except for one occasion, I never volunteered for anything while in the guard. The summer of 1954, a few from our unit were going to go to Fort Knox, Kentucky to train, while the remainder went to Indiantown Gap, Pennsylvania. A captain, I have forgotten his name, asked for a volunteer to be his jeep driver in Ft. Knox. I never drove a jeep before, but how hard could it be? At least I would know what I was doing.

The flight to Kentucky was my first time in an airplane. My seat belt would not stay fastened. One trait (failing?) is that I am reluctant to request help. Rather than ask anyone, I pushed the ends of the seat belt together so that it appeared fastened when the flight attendant checked. That may not be smart, but that is me.

When we arrived in Ft. Knox, I learned that I would not be a driver.

MEMOIRS AND MORE

The army was no longer allowing National Guardsmen to drive jeeps because they were involved in so many accidents. I was out of a job. This could be a stroke of luck and I would have nothing to do. On the other hand, if assigned to a tank I would have to play soldier for two weeks. For some unknown reason I bunked in the supply room with the supply sergeant instead of in the barracks with everyone else. The supply sergeant was a friend so that was okay with me. The first roll call was the following morning. The only name not called was mine. Is this a stroke of luck? Do they not know that I am here? On the other hand, they might know I am here but have no idea why. Either way this could turn out to be a good thing. For much of the two weeks I just hung out in the supply room. When I left the supply room, I held papers in my hand and walked purposely in order to appear to be delivering them. Nobody ever questioned me. The captain I expected to drive for did not seem to care what I did. One morning he let me ride with him to the range where they fired bazookas at a target tank. The tank never took a hit. I think they missed on purpose so the tankers lost any fear of bazooka fire. Another afternoon I got to ride around in a tank and learned how to communicate on the tank's radio.

    We had leave for the weekend. Four of us went to downtown Ft. Knox together. I played golf for the first time and made the longest (at least 50 feet) putt I ever made and no one saw it but me. We ate at a church that offered free dinners to service men then stayed at the YMCA. As far as I know that is all we did. Were we wild and crazy guys or what? When we got back to camp, nobody asked what we did. I'm glad. It would have been embarrassing to admit what we did (didn't) do.

    The following year, 1955, summer camp was at Indiantown Gap, Pennsylvania. I still did not have any idea what I was doing. There were maneuvers in the field just like those on television. Except, at mid-afternoon the Good Humor man came through selling ice cream. We spent several days in the field living and working in tents. After dark we lived and worked (I don't remember doing any work) under blackout conditions so that no light could be seen from outside. Since we were in the middle of a forest it was pitch dark. It was necessary to follow wires strung through the trees to get from one tent to another. One night I heard, "Halt! Who goes there, what's the password?" What password? Nobody told me about any password. If I could not see him, he could not see me. He did not have real bullets anyway. I just mumbled, "Damn if I know," (I really didn't know) and kept going. Had this been the real thing he could have shot me.

    Rather than waiting for the draft, I requested a transfer to active duty in order to get my military service obligation over with as soon as possible. I took my pre-induction physical at Fort Meade just before Christmas 1956. On my way home, I bought a Christmas tree for $20.00. This was an especially nice tree, but $20.00 was an enormous sum for a tree then. It must have been nerves.

    Lois became pregnant. Fathers were exempt from the draft so I never went on active duty. Since I never understood or saw any purpose in what I was doing, I took no pleasure in doing it. Had I asked, it is likely someone would have told me. When I do not understand something, my predisposition is to muddle through rather than ask and hope that things clear up. Nothing cleared up. Therefore, I left the guard when my enlistment was up. I still have mixed feelings about not serving in the military. A part of me feels that if others had to go, I should have gone also.

YOUTH GROUPS

I joined the Cub Scouts at Kenwood Presbyterian Church when I was about eight years old. It must have been for a very short time because I remember practically nothing. The Cub pack met periodically at the church. The individual dens met in homes between pack meetings. My mother was a den mother so my den met at our house. I have no idea what we did. The only activity I remember is sleeping in a large rustic cabin on an overnight camping trip.

I joined Company O of the Boys Brigade sometime after leaving Cub Scouts and before joining Boy Scouts. An internet search describes it as, "A Christian, Boy Scout like organization with a range of activities including games, sports, crafts and Christian activities." We met weekly at the Overlea Methodist Church. There were no religious or scout-like activities. It may be because we were in the middle of World War II, but it seems it was more military like than scout like. We did military type things. Our uniforms looked military; we carried wooden rifles, marched in parades and learned flag etiquette. We played Simon Says to practice the manual of arms. Some meeting nights we would have a sham battle, an army game played in the fields and woods behind where the Paramount Movie was and the Overlea Diner is now. Sports (e.g., iron horse, wrestling, and boxing) were associated with physical conditioning. I'm not a fighter, but boxing was okay because the gloves were almost as big as I was. Nobody got hurt. Jay Irwin, a school buddy, had a glass eye that he took out when boxing. Jay hit me a lot since I paid more attention to the empty eye socket than boxing.

I was twelve when I joined Boy Scout Troop 146 at St. James

MARVIN LEROY OED

Evangelical Lutheran Church in Overlea. Although Lois went to that church, we never crossed paths there. This was a very active troop thanks to an excellent scoutmaster, a Mr. Fenker, and a supportive minister, Pastor Freed. The Friday night meetings often focused on preparing to earn various merit badges. We collected and sold newspapers to raise money to pay for our camping activities.

The Jasper family owned a large piece of wooded property and allowed the scout troop use it. A building, resembling a garage, was erected and outfitted with a wood burning stove and bunks and was used all year round. One Friday, after a meeting, several scouts and an assistant scoutmaster left to spend the weekend there. Two friends, Howard Shores and Mason Clift, and I decided we would go also. Assuming we were going to become a part of this group, one of our parents drove us there. We had something else in mind. We did not go the cabin where everyone else was. We hiked to a lean-to we built on an earlier trip. Whether planned or a spur of the moment poor judgment, what we did to be funny was not funny at all. In the middle of the night, we walked from our lean-to to the cabin. Along the way we found a heavy log, just the right size to prop the only door shut. Not wanting those inside to know who we were none of us said a word. We propped the door shut with the log and then took sticks and ran around cabin dragging the sticks along the wall. This made quite a racket on the metal building. After a few minutes of this, we took the log away and went back to our lean-to. In the morning, when the other scouts learned it was us they were not happy about what we did. We scared the daylights out of them. The following week we heard about it from the scout leaders and the scout council. When our parents learned what happened we heard about it again at home. This was very poor judgment on our part. What were we thinking? Doing or saying anything that scares or hurts others is never funny. I am sorry this happened.

Each summer Troop 146 went to Gunpowder Youth Camp for a week. We were kept busy the entire week. Some of the time was devoted to working on earning merit badges. Scouting activities were interspersed with swimming, softball and other games. Many of the activities involved competition between the patrols. One of these was to build a fire, mix pancake batter, cook the pancake on one side, then flip it over a rope strung about seven or eight feet in the air, catch it and cook the other side. The first to eat the pancake was the winner. The secret was to make the batter very thick so it would hold together. The most difficult part was eating a thick, lumpy, undercooked pancake that may have fallen in the dirt. There was no butter or syrup to help. You never tasted anything quite like it. Another competition was to start a fire and be the first to boil a paper cup of water over it. A third was to start a fire with a spark created by striking flint and steel together. A variation of the flint and steel method involved using fire bow (looks like a miniature archers bow), a spindle stick (resembles a dowel), and a softwood base with a notch to accommodate the spindle stick. One end of the spindle stick goes in the notch. The bow, used like a hand drill, turns the spindle stick rapidly until the wood begins to glow. The spark created by the dowel is transferred to the tinder. If everything goes as planned, the tinder begins to blaze and starts the fire. I never had any luck starting a fire this way. The last contest used a fire started the real Boy Scout way, matches. The object is to build a fire and be the first to burn through a string stretched about three feet above the ground. To test our compass reading skills, an object hidden in the grass of a large open field had to be located by following an assigned compass reading. Another test was to follow a trail through the woods by following signs made from sticks or stones that indicated the direction we should go. Scout's pace is a timed trial of half walking and half jogging. The idea is to finish a measured mile in as near to twelve minuets as possible without using a watch. The competition was between the patrols and was intense but no scores were kept and no prizes given. The competition provided the fun, not winning or losing. Today it seems that winning is the only thing that counts. The experience with little league baseball, soccer, and basketball is that the kids are happy playing for fun but it is the parents and coaches who feel that winning is more important. The result is that when they should be having fun and learning the sport, the better players get the most attention. The others, who could benefit the most, play less and get less attention. Only the winners have fun and the others lose interest. Our way was better.

Parents visited Wednesday evening for a campfire program. Two friends, Howard Shores and Mason Clift, and I proposed a novel way to light the campfire and received permission to do so. We stacked the firewood in the usual pyramid. Then we fastened a string under the firewood, stretched it taut and attached it about twelve feet high in a nearby tree. A scorched piece of cloth attached to an "S" hook made from a wire clothes hanger was to be our fire starter. Our dry runs (the cloth unlit) proved that the hook and cloth would slide down the string and land in the tinder. On parent's night, one of us in the tree, invisible in the dark, would set the cloth on fire. The blazing cloth would slide down the string into the tinder and start the campfire. We thought this would be very dramatic. It was, but not as we expected. The "S" hook with the burning cloth began sliding down the string. Halfway down the flame burned through the string and the fiery cloth dropped to the ground. Fortunately, we had decided not to allow anyone to sit below the string. As a result, the only thing injured was our egos. It never occurred to us during our dry runs that the string might burn.

Adjacent to Gunpowder Youth Camp was Camp Puh'Toh. As we had scouting activities, Puh'Toh had Indian activities. Each year we went there to watch Indian dances and other ceremonies. One boy had a pet snake and performed a dance with it. Later that evening we learned that snake died earlier that afternoon and he performed with his dead pet.

In 1948, we went to Broad Creek Scout Camp instead of Gunpowder because Mr. Fenker was ill. This is a much larger facility. There are multiple campsites and several scout troops there at the same time. Everyone in our group wrote home complaining. Usually it was because we thought the leader ran the camp like the marine drill sergeant he was and the food was terrible. He was away one night and everyone went amok. We went to another group's campsite and pulled the tent pegs out of the ground so their tents collapsed.

One night there was a thunderstorm. We had about two inches of water running through our tent. Since we slept on cots, our only concern was getting our belongings off the ground. The tents were in a circle around the flagpole. Lightening struck the flagpole. Those of us touching any metal part of the cot got a shock. It was funny at the time. Later that day we learned that lighting killed several cows standing under a nearby tree.

In my mother's scrapbook is a letter I wrote to my father. It is signed, "The Gang, Marvin, Howard, Richard and Mason" and asking him to bring $5.01 so we could buy three tee shirts. This is somewhat of a mystery. Why would four people sign a letter to my father? Why order three tee shirts since there were four people?

In July of 1950, Valley Forge, Pennsylvania hosted the first World Wide Boy Scout Jamboree in the United States. Howard Shores, Mason Clift, John Dorsey and I were the four from Troop 146 in the Maryland contingent. Everyone in the Maryland group met in Herring Run Park for an orientation and job assignments. I volunteered for and shared the job of cook with a boy from another troop. This was great. I liked to cook and that was the only thing we would have to do. Before meals, other scouts picked up the food. We cooked it and our job was over. After meals, others cleaned up, washed the pots and pans and disposed of the garbage. The cooks watched.

We arrived at Valley Forge to learn that our tents would not be there until the next day. We slept on the ground in the open the first night. There was no rain so this was not a problem. In fact, this added to the ambiance of the experience. Early the next day our equipment arrived and we set up our tents, etc. While setting up out tent, I discovered a potential "wardrobe malfunction." All the scouts at the jamboree wore identical uniforms. These were similar to my regular uniform except for the short pants instead of long. The last time I wore short pants was when I was about six years old. My grandmother made my boxer underwear. I never thought about them presenting a problem. I stooped to drive a tent peg into the ground. Glancing down, I very quickly realized that boxer shorts are not suitable with short pants. Nobody saw anything but me. I had no jockey shorts and no place to buy any. I was very careful about my posture all week and made it through without embarrassment.

There were 45,000 scouts from around the world camped on the same parade ground where the continental army marched in the 1700's. Both President Truman and General Eisenhower spoke one evening. This was the same week that North Korea invaded South Korea. I don't remember what they said, but recently read that Truman spoke about furthering brotherhood while Eisenhower damned the invasion and hinted at U.S. intervention. Can you imagine any president today speaking to a group this large, in an open area, and with no visible security precautions? Times have changed.

There was a great deal of interaction and trading of souvenirs with scouts from many of the states and a number of foreign countries. There was a trip to Philadelphia to visit the Liberty Bell. This is where I first heard about "snipe" hunting. I guessed this to be some sort of trick. To avoid being tricked I acted as though I knew what a snipe hunt was. One scout, who did not know became the mark. Told that participating in his first snipe hunt is an honor, he willingly agreed. Later that night we walked to a dark, wooded area of Valley Forge Park. Someone described a snipe to him as a small bird that did not fly but ran along the ground and was unable to bite or hurt anyone. Our job was to go into the woods to drive the snipes toward him. His job was to stay in place and scoop snipes into a burlap bag as they ran by. He was standing there in the dark holding a burlap bag when we left. I wish that I could recall what happened but the outcome is a blank in my memory. Did he catch on and follow us back? Maybe he is he still there waiting the snipes to come running.

The last night before we left all the tents came down. All 45,000 scouts slept on the ground. It was pitch black and impossible to see your hand in front of your face. The dark was not a deterrent but made it a challenge to get around. Someone yelled (or, maybe it he cursed). The beginning of the week each campsite dug a hole about a foot in diameter and several feet deep. This is where the fat and grease was disposed of after cooking. One job the final night was filling the "grease pits" with dirt. Someone roaming in the dark accidently stepped into an unfilled grease pit. Imagine being up to your knee in this week old mess. It was funny, but would not have been had it been me.

I liked scouting in general but loved every minute of the camping part. I made the rank of Life Scout and was on my way to be coming an Eagle Scout.

SIXTEEN=DRIVER'S LICENSE=GIRLS

As a young teenager, I belonged to the youth groups at the Kenwood Presbyterian Church and the Overlea Methodist Church. This provided my first experiences going out with girls. Initially it was group activities rather than dating. There were also class parties and private parties. The Overlea Recreation Center held dances on Saturday nights. A few people came as dates. I went stag and hoped to be able to walk some girl home. It never happened; I was too shy to ask. After the dance, I usually walked to the Overlea Diner with friends and got a hamburger and french fries with gravy.

In 1950, I got my driver's license and lost some of my shyness. Now I had the potential use of a car and could ask a girl on a real date. Instead of going to boy scouts, I went scouting for girls. My quest for Eagle Scout ended. Eagle Scout is a commendable achievement. Now and then it crosses my mind that I could and should have both dated and become an Eagle Scout.

In 1951, still in scouts, I joined DeMolay, a junior Masonic organization. There was no interest in the rituals but I had friends who belonged and I liked the activities. There were conventions and dances in downtown hotels. I took Lois to the dances. She was crowned Queen at a dance held at the Lord Baltimore Hotel. I played softball and Lois came to watch. Much later, I learned that Lois does not care for sports. Could she have had an ulterior motive?

The 1940's and 50's was a much kinder, gentler and more civil era than those that followed. Parents allowed children to be children longer. That allowed us to mature as we aged. Today's children are pushed to grow up. They age but do not mature. We grew up a little slower but a lot wiser because time allowed us to mature. Boy/girl relationships developed gradually. First came group activities where boys and girls got together but not as couples. This allowed boys and girls to get to know each other in a somewhat protected environment. Churches had youth groups, the county had recreation centers, schools had class activities and parties, etc. We would go skating, biking or bowling etc. in small groups. School dances were chaperoned. We had a few dances in junior high school. Some came as couples and others, perhaps most, came stag. Boys and girls began to develop social skills.

High school dances were more frequent and almost everyone came as couples. The first time a boy asked a girl out (a girl never asked a boy out) it was probably to a school dance or a movie. There was no commitment. Dating more than one boy or one girl was the norm. Dating just one person was a serious decision. Going steady required a very serious decision. Giving a girl a school ring or a friendship ring was very special.

Everything changes at age sixteen when a teenager gets a driver's license and access to a car. The parents lose control of where their children go and what they do. What they instilled in us is what guided us. I believe we were much better prepared to handle our new freedoms. We were too young to buy beer but would pitch in and find someone to buy it for us. Loch Raven was a favorite spot for a weekend beer party. We drank beer because we knew we shouldn't. It is never a good idea to drink and drive but I do not remember anyone getting drunk. I was not aware of any other drug use. More than one can of beer made me uncomfortable. To maintain an image, I would drink part of the can of beer, empty the remainder on the ground and go back for another. Was this peer pressure? This was in the woods, in the dark and plenty of cars available. However, as far as I know, the activities there were limited to socializing.

Parents told children that smoking would stunt their growth. The real dangers were unknown then. I did smoke, but only occasionally.

I guess it was because, "That's what adults did." I never particularly cared for it. Once in college, I changed to a pipe because I thought it made me appear intellectual. When managing Rutkowski's Pharmacy I went back to cigarettes. I only smoked the free cigarettes that the sales representatives left. It is fortunate that I never developed a taste for cigarettes. One day I decided it was senseless to smoke just because the cigarettes were free. I have not smoked a cigarette since. Now it is an occasional cigar with my brother-in-law Tedd. Until Tedd developed an allergy to crabs, the cigar was along with steamed crabs and beer. Now it is just for old time's sake. We look like Denny Crane and Alan Schorr of *Boston Legal* on their balcony.

Blaming "peer pressure" for smoking, drinking, drugs, etc. is an excuse, not the cause. There was no pressure to drink or smoke. I did it because drinking and smoking is what adults did. Drugs, other than alcohol, were virtually unknown to me. I heard that criminals and jazz musicians used marijuana but never knew anyone who did.

The moral expectation of the 1950's was that the accepted order of events was dating, engagement and marriage. Then sex and children followed. Today there is no order. I am not so naive to believe that everyone conformed to the expectations. I do believe the constraints of the day gave us more time to mature and deal with these issues more rationally than emotionally.

My perception of boys' attitudes came from what I know about myself and surmised from what I heard from male friends. When hormones kicked in, thoughts about sex crept (or leapt) in. My perceptions of girl's attitudes are from what Lois has told me. Interest in sex began as curiosity and developed gradually. First, it was kissing games at parties. Necking, usually in a car at Lake Montebello or Loch Raven reservoir, came later. Nobody talked about anything beyond that. It was private if/when, something more occurred. It seems very little is private today.

Boys thought of sex as a sport and not as having anything to do with a relationship or love. Boys bragged (more often, lied) about their sexual exploits. Lois told me that girls looked for the "right" someone to date. Not for sex, but for someone who cared about her and with whom she would like to develop a relationship. The interest and desire for a sexual relationship came much later. Boys wanted sex. Girls said no. That was their job. A boy who had sex had "sown his wild oats" and the issue forgotten. A girl in the same situation would have gotten a "reputation." This was a double standard but it served a useful purpose. It encouraged girls say no to boys. Just saying no worked then because of the social barriers. Values of the day said that marriage should come before sex. Birth control pills were non-existent so pregnancy was a real possibility. A pregnant girl might not be allowed to attend high school or graduate with her class. Her parents might send her to "visit an aunt" in another city. An unwed mother was looked down on. Unmarried fathers had a financial responsibility to their children. It was not an option for an unmarried couple to live together. Marriage was the only viable option. Most of us married shortly after high school or college, much earlier than is usual today. This meant there was less time for pre-marital sex.

 The discovery and availability of birth control pills was the primary factor leading to changing sexual attitudes. Societal standards became more open-minded but the people less thoughtful. The combination resulted in a more casual attitude toward sex and to consequences that frequently are not for the better.

DATING GIRLS TO DATING A GIRL

I first met Lois, sort of, shortly after I started Kenwood High School. Dick Greaves, a friend from Fullerton School went to Baltimore Polytechnic. Each year they put on a show, *"The Poly Follies."* Poly was an all boy's school. Boys played both the male and female roles. Most noteworthy, the boys performing the can-can were almost as perfect as the Rockettes. Dick invited Howard and me to go with him. He picked us up and a few minutes later, much to our surprise, he picked up his date. Howard and I were bewildered to say the least. We had no idea he was going to take a date. Suave person that he was, Dick did purchase seats in different sections of the auditorium. Howard and I sat together and he sat with Lois. Lois and I were only together in the car. She was in the front, Howard and I in the back. There was little interaction so this does not really count as meeting Lois. I am not even sure Dick introduced us.

The first real meeting for Lois and me was in 1951 at my Kenwood High School Junior prom. Auts Ruff and I were friends. She went with Auts and I took Betty Wockenfuss. Later we saw each other at the Fullerton Recreation Center dances. I remembered Lois from my Junior Prom. We danced at the Overlea Recreation Center but never dated. One evening she came to the dance with her friend, Naomi Bourdon. Naomi looked like a cheerleader, bleached her hair platinum, smoked and probably even drank. Remember now, this was the 1950's; a goodnight kiss on the first date was a big deal. This could be an indication of a wild girl. She was not. However, I did not know that at the time. My plan was to talk to Lois and get to know Naomi. Who knows, I might get lucky. I was too shy or too dumb to make a direct

MEMOIRS AND MORE

approach. Lois did introduce me to Naomi. What happened was not what I anticipated. For some reason I ignored Naomi and asked Lois to go to a movie. I don't remember if I kissed Lois on our first date or not. I liked dating and dated nice girls before (never found the kind I was looking for) but never developed any special feelings toward any of them. I didn't realize it at the time but after my first date with Lois my life changed forever. Any romantic feeling from then on focused on her. I did not know it at the time but the feelings were mutual. Lois had been dating Phil Storm. Once Lois dumped Phil, (her parents really liked him) neither of us dated anyone else. We never decided to "go steady" it just happened. Lois and I had been dating for quite a while when I related the Poly Follies story. That was when I learned that she was the girl, and she learned that I was one of the boys in the back seat on her strange date that evening.

We went to my Kenwood High School Senior Prom and 1952 and to her Eastern High School Senior Prom in 1954. Things began getting serious.

We dated throughout college, frequently going to fraternity dances. Usually they were semi-formal affairs, held at a downtown hotel with a big band orchestra. Little Italy restaurants stayed open late and were favorite places to go after a dance. I ate spaghetti that did not come out of a can for the first time. It did take a few dinners before I became accustomed to the smell of the cheese. Most Sundays I ate supper with Lois at her home. Her aunt and uncle, Mildred and Lee Fait, were usually there also.

After taking Lois home from a date or spending the evening watching TV at the Davidson's, Harry and Edna would leave us and go to bed. Sometimes it seemed as though six shoes dropped. Eventually it dawned on me, this was a signal that it was time for me to leave. I didn't. Edna said that Harry asked, "What are they doing down there?" Edna's reply was, "The same thing we used to do." Harry responded, "I'll kill the SOB!"

I proposed in 1954. This was not a formal proposal, in a romantic setting, on bended knee and offering a ring. We were on the streetcar, on our way to school. My words were more an ultimatum than a proposal. I remember saying something like, "You have to marry me." It may have been unromantic but it was effective. The following Christmas Eve I gave her an engagement ring. Lois completed the X-Ray Technician program at University Hospital and graduated in 1955. I graduated from pharmacy school the following year.

Lois accepted a job with Dr. Herbert Copeland, a radiologist. She did not wear her engagement ring to the interview fearing it would hinder her chances for the job. Employers often assumed engaged women were likely to get married, become pregnant and leave their jobs. In fact, we did get married, Lois did become pregnant the following year and she did leave her job in X-Ray for safety reasons.

Sometimes ignorance is bliss. Asking Lois to marry me was not a conscious decision. All I knew was that we were in love and I wanted to marry her. It was the smartest thing I ever did. I cannot imagine a better marriage. We are alike in some ways and differ in others. Rather than cause conflict, our differences complement each other and I am better for it. Sometimes we disagree, but we have never had a real argument or fight. There is no reason to fight. My philosophy is that if unimportant, it is not worth fighting over. On the other hand, if important, no amount of fighting should cause me to change my mind. I Love my children as much as Lois does. However, she is much more nurturing than I am. Lois is less daring while I am confident that everything will work out.

I learned from a sermon that two things not to worry about are those I can do something about and those that I cannot. If I can do something, I should do it. If I cannot, worrying will not change it. Lois is much more likely to worry, so I let her do my worrying for me. She seems to prefer things to remain the same. I like change. We both tend to accede to the other's wishes.

Lois and I were married at St. James Evangelical Lutheran Church in Overlea just one week after I graduated from the University of

Maryland at Baltimore School of Pharmacy. I chose my father as my best man. The ushers were Ronald Mueller (cousin) and Walter Oster, Tedd Pruss, and Gregory Sophocleus (pharmacy school classmates). Lois's sister Carole was her maid of honor. Her sister Janice and close friend Ann Thieme were the bridesmaids. We were so in love it never crossed either of our minds that our love and marriage was anything but forever. We may have been naïve, but it turned out to be accurate. We are as much, or more, in love now as we were then.

Following the reception at the Davidson's home, we had dinner at the Candlelight Lodge in Catonsville and spent the night at our apartment on Barbara Avenue. The following day was Fathers Day. We surprised both our fathers by visiting them before driving to Paradise Valley Lodge, a honeymoon resort in the Pocono Mountains. There we met George and Eleanor Mill, from Philadelphia. During our three days there, we became friends and remain so today.

The following year we took a trip through Canada with Joe and Anne Thieme and stopped at Paradise Valley Lodge on our return. The management did not seem particularly pleased. Maybe it was because Lois was obviously pregnant at the time.

Lois and I chose to marry each other. However, no one has a choice of in-laws. We were fortunate there was never an in-law problem. Edna and Harry accepted me as a son. Equally important, my parents and my grandparents accepted Lois as a daughter and grandaughter. It was particularly nice that our parents became friends. The often celebrated holidays and went out together.

Edna was an excellent cook. My mother always cooked roast beef very well done. I was aghast when Edna served it rare. She knew that and always gave me the first slice. It was still rare but if turned upside down at least the top was brown. It only took a dinner or two to convince me that rare was much, much better. Edna continued to offer me that first slice. The first slice off a rare roast beef is still my favorite cut of meat. Once I said I liked something, it would be there the next time I came. Sometimes it seemed like it was there every time I came. She always tried to please me. Edna was a little unhappy when we left St. James Church Lutheran Church and began going to a Presbyterian church. Once she found out I was actively participating in the church she accepted it.

Harry would tolerate anything I did except if I mistreated Lois. We got along well and became very close. He was a rabid Baltimore Colt football fan and had season tickets from the day the team came to town. Lois had a 21st birthday party for me on a Saturday night. The Colts played that night. Harry had never missed a game since the Colts came to Baltimore until my party that night. This was the only game he ever missed and he never said a word about it. Later on, we went to the Colts games together. Major league baseball came to Baltimore in 1954 when the St. Louis Browns moved here. Harry's position with the White Tower chain got us a front row seat for the parade. We climbed a ladder to the roof of their restaurant at Howard and Centre Streets to watch as the motorcade with the Orioles, Maryland dignitaries and Vice President Nixon drove by on their way to Memorial Stadium. We did not go to the game but the Orioles won their first game in Baltimore by beating the Chicago White Sox, 3 to 1.

I am among the mechanically challenged. Lawnmowers in particular seem to know it. I would wear my arm out trying to start my lawnmower with no results. Then I would call Harry. He would do exactly what I did and it would start right off. It seemed he could fix anything electrical or mechanical. All I had to do was ask. Harry was willing to help almost anyone. However, pretend to know something when you did not and you would get little or no help at all. His humor sometimes rubbed people the wrong way. He knew just what to say to provoke a reaction. The thing to do was ignore it. If he knew it bothered you, it only encouraged him. We got along well together, never had an argument and had a close relationship from the very beginning.

Harry had a special knack of dealing with his grandchildren that made them feel much older than they were. A special treat for the boys was going to Hazelwood Inn with him, sitting at the bar, and having a hamburger and coke. They still remember going there.

Charlie Richeson, a friend for years, told me he was selling his wooden outboard runabout. Lois told me Harry always said he wanted a boat. I called and told him. Without asking for any details he said, "Let's buy it." We bought the runabout. That started a boating partnership that lasted a number of years. We had a lot of fun fishing, but not much luck catching. One morning, after a big storm, I went to Beacon Light Marina to check on our boat. It was a little difficult to find because it was about two feet under water. There was no automatic bilge pump to remove the rainwater and it was sitting on the bottom. The marina pulled it out, put it on blocks and drilled a hole in the bottom to let the water out. We kept the motor and sold the boat. Who would want a boat without a motor and a hole in the bottom?

Our second boat was a snazzy fifteen-foot fiberglass runabout with a canvas top. This was the best looking of the four boats that we owned. However, a boat without a head might be fine for the two of us but was not practical for women. One summer we took it with us when we stayed at a Cabin in Elk Neck State Park.

We traded the runabout for an eighteen-foot boat with a cuddy cabin that had a head. Douglas was not born yet so we named this the "*El Gee*" for Leslie and Gregory. Harry and I joined the Bush River Yacht Club and kept this boat there.

Boaters seem to buy increasingly larger boats. Our fourth, and final, boat was a twenty-seven foot Concord with a flying bridge, galley and head. This one we called "The King and I." We never discussed it but Harry thought he was the king and I thought I was. We had a lot of fun fishing, sometimes staying overnight. The boat was bigger but no better at catching fish. Boating is frequently an adventure. At Miller's Island, a spark plug blew out of the engine because the dealer sold us the wrong one. Near the Bay Bridge, a crab trap floated loose and wrapped around the propeller. I spent about an hour up to my neck in sea nettles untangling it. Another time, while taking a nap, the exhaust pipe came loose at the transom and water flooded the bilge. It is a good thing it was just a short nap. Had we been asleep for the night we might have floated out of our bunks. Once we stayed overnight at a marina at the east end of the Bay Bridge. The following morning, while trolling, the propeller shaft cracked apart just where it entered the engine. We were able to force it back in and made back to the marina for repairs. One afternoon while sailing toward the bay bridge, one blade of the three-blade propeller broke off. The boat vibrated a lot, but we continued to run very slowly, and made it to the same marina that fixed the propeller shaft a year or so earlier. The replaced the propeller. The Bush River is deep enough so that few boaters bother to follow the channel buoys. Coming back to the yacht club in the dark I ran into the only rock pile in Bush River and damaged the propeller. I took a lot of razzing at the yacht club. Apparently, everyone but me knew about this rock pile. I was lucky. The ruined propeller was not good but had it been low tide the rock pile would have put a hole in the hull. Boating was frequently an adventure.

After a few years it seemed we used the boat more because we felt we should, in order to get our moneys worth, rather than because we wanted to. We sold the King and I and were out of boating. There is a saying, "The two best days in a sailor's life are the day he buys his boat and the day he sells it." Now and then, I get a feeling that it would be nice to have a boat again. I flush a few hundred dollars down the toilet and the feeling goes away.

NEVER FAR FROM HOME

We now live in Cockeysville, Maryland, about fifteen miles from Overlea. This is the farthest I've ever lived from where I was born. Our first home was a one-bedroom, second floor apartment in a house on Barbara Avenue in Gardenville. The owners, Bernard and Thelma Thanner, were nice and we became friends. The location was the last house on the street and adjacent to a wooded area. While we were living there, I began giving Lois driving lessons. Actually, I gave Lois one driving lesson. She did very well. When Lois got into the car for the second lesson she said, "Which one's the brake?" I said, "Call a driving school." She did and earned her license without a problem.

When Lois became pregnant, we decided we needed more room and should buy a house. In July of 1957, we moved to Hilltop Avenue in the Overlea/Hamilton. My cousin and her husband were moving out of town and we bought their home. On moving day, I worked. Lois, pregnant at the time, and her mother handled the entire move. That was unfair. I should have planned better.

Gregory and Leslie were born a year apart while we lived on Hilltop Avenue. This was a good move. The neighborhood was relatively new so there were many people our age there.

Gregory was born in Sinai Hospital on November 26, 1957. In the waiting room, I met a friend from high school, also waiting for his first child. He showed me pictures of his wife. He had several pictures, all posed naked. What should I have said to a man about his naked wife? "Nice boobs" did not seem to be appropriate. I did not know what to say then and I do not know now. Leslie was born in the same hospital on December 30, 1958.

MARVIN LEROY OED

Lois' Aunt Mildred arrived for lunch to find Lois trying to find Leslie. They searched and searched with no luck. They were about to call the police they found Leslie asleep in her toy box. They overlooked her many times because Gregory had covered her with stuffed toys. Gregory and Leslie were about three and four years old when I built a Christmas garden for them. The houses, zoo, train, figures, etc. were from my Christmas garden as a child. My Christmas garden, at their age, was only to look at. This was for them to play with. They rearranged the people and the buildings. The animals, freed from the zoo, rode around in the train along with the people. I assume they were trying to reroute the train but only managed to pull up the track.

We had no clothes dryer. Lois hung wash outside to dry. There were no disposable diapers then. With two babies in cloth diapers, it was time to buy a dryer. I made a hole through the concrete foundation for the dryer vent. That was quite a task by hand using a hammer and star chisel.

Janice, Lois's sister, and her boyfriend, Richard Scheler, often baby sat for us. They married in 1962. I guess we can take some credit for furthering their romance. Richard helped me with a very messy job; patching a water leak in the basement wall. We dug a trench the length of the wall, wide enough for us to stand in and deep enough to reach the base of the foundation. The messy part was covering the wall with tar. When finished, we looked like walking licorice sticks. Later, on Hamiltowne Circle, Richard stepped in when I got disgusted attempting to wallpaper a bathroom. I quit. He and Lois finished it.

The Hilltop Improvement Association was very active and brought the neighborhood together. Before Christmas, Santa Clause visited every house and gave each child a present. There were occasional outings and a yearly Halloween dance. Each year there was an Easter egg hunt in Burdick Park. It took a group of us several hours to hide the sixty dozen eggs that Lois helped dye. The kids lined up, a whistle blew and the hunt was on. What took hours and hours to prepare for was over in about ten minutes.

We made many friends there, several of whom we still see. Charles and Eleanor Richeson moved in just a block away. Lois had not seen Eleanor since they were in Eastern High School together. We were close friends for many years, and have remained friends with Charles since Eleanor passed away. We are very close with Harold and Dolores Schweitzer. It has been over fifty years and we still play cards, take day trips and go to dances together. Getting together is easy now that they moved a few minutes away in Timonium.

We are close friends with Carolyn and Ernie Ilgenfritz. Lois knew Carolyn in kindergarten and I met them shortly after we married. We vacationed several times with them in the Florida Keys, their vacation cabin in the mountains, and shore homes in Secretary and Crisfield Maryland.

With one exception, none of my friends ever sought business from me. Likewise, I never solicited them for business. The exception, the husband of a couple we played bridge with, ended a friendship. The husband sold life insurance and asked me to let him review my policies, a typical ploy to sell insurance. I was not interested in more insurance and told him I was not going to buy any more. He insisted he only wanted to "review my coverage to make sure everything was in order." He asked a few questions and took the policies with him. When he came back he began by saying something to the effect that based on what I said, I needed several hundred thousand dollars more life insurance. I was extremely annoyed, to say the least, he was taking advantage of a friendship.

The conversation went something like:
HIM: "How much do you want to buy now?"
ME: "None."
HIM: "But, you said…"
ME: "I told you I wasn't going to buy more insurance."
HIM: "If you died you wouldn't want Lois to have to go to work, would you?"
ME: "If I have to die the least Lois can do is go to work."

Lois intervened before the situation deteriorated any more. We never invited them to play bridge again. In contrast, another friend, Ron Resch changed jobs and began selling insurance. He never said anything regarding insurance, other than that it was his new job. I respected him for that and bought all my business insurance from him from then on. Later he told me that when he started with State Farm they wanted a list of family and friends so they could send a letter soliciting insurance. He refused to provide it. That is character. We are close friends to this day.

I dislike sales gimmicks. A photo studio came door-to-door asking to take children's pictures for a "contest." The winner was to get a number of photographs taken free. Lois let him take pictures of Gregory and Leslie. He came back when I was home and Lois was not. I asked if we won. He said no, and tried to sell me pictures. I told him I was not interested. Lois was very unhappy with me. She really wanted those photographs and thought I should know that. She should have told me. I'm a man, I'm not psychic. Subtle hint don't work, broad hints don't work, you have to tell me.

After five years on Hilltop Avenue, we decided to build a house. We moved to Hamilton Circle in Rosedale in July of 1963 just after Gregory completed kindergarten. At the time, we were the last house in the development. The only thing next to us was empty lots. We left the living room empty and used the clubroom while deciding on new furniture.

Douglas was born in Sinai Hospital in 1970. Dr. Muher let me witness the Delivery. I was a comfort for Lois and therefore glad I was there. Watching the actual delivery doesn't help anyone. I don't understand why families want to watch or why a mother-to-be would want an audience.

John F. Kennedy was assassinated on November 22, 1963. Two days later, we watched as Jack Ruby shot and killed Lee Harvey Oswald as the Dallas police transferred Oswald from the Police Department to the county jail. November 23, 1963 John F. Kennedy's funeral was on television. We heard gunshots that we thought were part of the ceremony. Lois thought they sounded nearby and looked out the window. There were two hunters on the empty lot next to our house. They told Lois they were after a fox. She expressed concern that they were a danger to our children and us. They left right away.

The following summer we were playing bridge in the clubroom and heard fire engines. They sounded close so we walked upstairs to see. I saw the firemen tramping across my vegetable garden to put out a fire on the lot next door. I knew immediately that I was responsible and decided the best thing was to say nothing. The empty lot was all weeds. I tried cutting them with the lawn mower but it was too difficult. Then I got I got a bright, or maybe not so bright, idea. It would be easier to burn the weeds. That afternoon Roy Hale, the neighbor behind us, and I started a small fire and burned some of the weeds. When done, we put the fire out with a garden hose. Just to be sure, I left the water sprinkler on to saturate the area. Obviously, it was not adequate. No firemen came to the door and no one ever asked any questions so I never had to explain what happened.

Rosedale was more rural then and just beginning to be developed. One day Gregory, Leslie and I walked along where Interstate 95 is now and encountered overgrowth so thick we could not go any further. There was a derelict car in the underbrush and we could not figure out how it got there.

The house was on what once was an onion farm. There was not a single tree on the lot. Lois loves trees. We began planting (actually, Lois pointed to the spot and I planted) them. There were trees in the front yard, the side yards, and over the entire back yard. Eventually, the entire house was in shade. Some of the neighbors began calling Lois the "tree lady."

A few years later, we built a ground level deck around one of the trees. The trees and the deck gave us privacy where we entertained and ate many of our evening meals. I liked having my morning coffee on the deck.

Lois' parents gave us a catalpa tree seedling from their yard. Seedlings from our tree are now growing in Gregory's yard. A branch broke off a weeping willow tree in a neighbor's yard. They gave us the branch and we planted in our back yard. Soon was a full-grown tree. The branches hung to the ground making a little room under the tree. One day Leslie gathered her stuffed animals and said she was going to run away from home. She spent the rest of the afternoon under the weeping willow and came in when Lois called her for dinner.

We had two wedding receptions at our home on Hamiltowne Circle. Shortly after we moved Tedd and Lois's sister, Carole, held their reception there. The first was when Tedd and Carole used the first floor and basement clubroom for their wedding reception. The living room was unfurnished; we were waiting for our new furniture to arrive. This gave the caterer an open space to set up. Guests in the clubroom forgot they were in a home. After the reception, we found that cigarettes extinguished on the floor instead of put in ashtrays. Apparently, men put their feet us as they leaned against the wall and left shoe prints. We repainted.

In 1956, Gregory and Cheryl held their wedding reception at our house. The reception was nearly a disaster. I went to pick up the food from the caterer and found they had closed early. I went to a delicatessen a few doors away to see if they could fix something, anything, quick. When I told them may story they said, "Oh we have your order, when they close early they leave it here." A sign in the window or a phone call would have been helpful.

Bill and Marty Rorke owned a grocery store just a block away. We became good friends. I mentioned that it would be nice to have a family room. Bill, who has a lot of experience in this area said, "We can build one." We did. I know how to use the tools but need direction. Therefore, Bill was in charge and I was his helper. Ever helpful when needed, Harry took care of the electrical wiring and the air conditioner.

MEMOIRS AND MORE

Gregory, Cheryl and Leslie bought a two apartment house. Leslie lived on the second floor while Gregory, Cheryl and Danielle lived on the first. We purchased Gregory and Cheryl's half interest in the house when they moved. Our intent was to rent the apartment. We thought that with Leslie there the problems would be minimal. Boy, were we wrong. What were we thinking? Tenants, even those we knew, left a terrible mess when they moved out. Many never paid the rent for the last month.

A mess is bad enough, but one tenant installed grow lights and a watering system in a closet and was raising marijuana. I asked him to leave after I learned that strange people came to his door at all hours of the day and night. Alternatively, a car horn would blow and out he would come. Then there would be a transaction through the car window. To say he left the apartment in complete disarray is a colossal understatement. I filled ten large trash bags with empty liquor bottles that were lying around. The carpets had many cigarette burns. I did not find a square foot without at least several burns, most, had many more. Only good fortune kept him from burning the house down. There were several bags of fertilizer stored in the attic. He had partially insulated the attic and there was enough material there to finish the job. It was evident that he planned to expand his marijuana business. BGE turned his electric off after he failed to pay his bill. He left food in the freezer. It apparently rotted while the electric was off. The electric was on when he moved out but the rotten food was still in the freezer. He left, leaving his car parked at the curb. Eventually the city towed it away.

Another tenant left on short notice. He left a pile of wrapped Christmas presents for his child as well as toys his child played with when he visited. He owned a restaurant and left commercial steam trays and pans, as well as large jars of pickles. We now use the steam trays as roasting pans.

One couple moved out and took all the venetian blinds with them. Another left after Leslie said she would call the police if she heard him beating his wife again.

Leslie was on the front porch watching a tenant putting things in his pickup truck. They had become friends and she kiddingly said, "Are you moving out?" He said, "Yes" and drove away. He left some of his furniture and never came back.

Enough is enough. We got out and Leslie is now the sole owner of the house. Her brother, Douglas, rents the apartment. That seems to be working out for both of them.

I turned fifty in 1984. The "big 50" does not seem so big anymore. I think birthday parties are okay for kids, up to about twelve. I can make an exception for sixteen and twenty-one. With sixteen comes a driver's license and at twenty-one the right to vote and drink legally. Although I never thought of fifty as being special, Lois apparently did. However, I especially dislike surprise parties. For reasons still unfathomable to me, Lois decided to give me a surprise party. Later she told me she was afraid I would find out and not come home for dinner. She was probably right. Fearing I would turn around and leave if I saw people, she blocked the driveway with her car forcing me to park on the street. Consistent with my usual powers of observation, I failed to notice the inordinate number of cars parked nearby and walked right past one friend's distinctive red, white and blue van without noticing anything unusual. I was three quarters of the way down the driveway before becoming aware of all the people. Gregory, Leslie and Douglas helped with the preparation. I do appreciate the effort required but never understood the surprise aspect. As far as I know, no one but Lois knows about my feeling regarding birthday parties in general and surprise birthday parties in particular.

Cockeysville is as far as Lois and I ever moved from our homes in Overlea. We were friendly with our next-door neighbor on Hamiltowne Circle for fifteen years. Branches of our trees began growing over his fence making it difficult for him to mow. I understood why he trimmed them. Then he began complaining more and more about our trees. One branch was weak and going to fall on his car and another was going to drop on his fence. His telephone line was close to a branch that was going to pull the wire off from his house. The power line was close to a tree trunk and if it touched the tree the electric could come down to the ground and electrocute him. Both the telephone company and the gas and electric companies investigated and told him there was no problem. I hired an arborist who said the tree branches were okay. In an effort to pacify him, I had braces put on the two branches he mentioned. He continued trimming the branches hanging over his fence higher and higher. Over time, every branch on his side of the fence up to about twenty-five feet was gone. Why so high? I did not understand but as long as it was his side of the fence, I didn't care. The complaints never stopped. Then he wanted a branch extending over his storage shed trimmed because birds perched there and messed on the roof. The final straw came when he topped three trees on my side of the fence and trimmed every branch off so they looked like three twelve foot telephone poles. Lois saw the three trees and became semi-hysterical. I called him and told him to cut off any thing he wanted on his side of the fence, but to stay off my property and not to touch anything on my side of the fence. His response was to threaten to smash my cars with a baseball bat if anything fell on his property. We went to the police. They could do nothing because he threatened my cars, not me. We would have to wait until he damaged the cars before the police could become involved.

Lois said something to the effect, "That's it, we're moving." I had been ready to move for several years but thought this was just temporary anger for Lois. Two days later, I overheard a telephone conversation and Lois saying, "We're moving." That was all I needed. I am not a fighter and my neighbor was not going to change. We began looking for an apartment and put the house up for sale. The house sold in less than a week. We had scheduled a two-week cruise before the closing. Concerned what might happen during the time we were gone, I asked him for a list of all the things he wanted done and said would contact my arborist. The intent was to keep him from doing any cutting while I was away. I knew that nothing listed was necessary and asked the arborist to indicate that for each item. I had no intent of doing anything. His last hurrah was to report to the real estate board that there was a dispute between neighbors. The seller is then required to tell any prospective buyer about such a dispute. The sale was completed but we had not settled. I walked the property with the buyer and compared everything on Gary's list with the arborists report. The sale went through and I breathed a sigh of relief.

There was one last hurdle. There was a window between the living room and family room. The reason I never closed it when building the room is a mystery. It was not apparent because a mirror covered the living room side and shelves were on the family room side. In our bedroom, instead of dismantling the headboard when I painted I just painted as far as I could reach. The new buyers were not aware of either. I arranged for Chip Plantholt to come as soon as our furniture was gone to close up the window and paint the living room and bedroom walls.

We were very happy in Rosedale for forty of the forty-one years we were there. It is regrettable that we left under these circumstances.

Lois and I decided to look north of Baltimore City between Belair and York Roads for an apartment with two bedrooms and a den. The response we heard most often was "We don't have one of those available right now, check again in three months." With the house sold, we did not have three months. By chance, we directed to Briarcliff East. They had one apartment that was available immediately and it exceeded our requirements. It was available immediately. This apartment had amenities that we liked but rarely saw elsewhere. It did not face a parking lot, was on an upper floor, the balcony overlooked a wooded area and golf course, the laundry facilities are within the apartment, the storage area is off our balcony, and there is daily trash removal from the front door. The pool and gym were nice but were inconsequential at that time. They turned out to be important my diagnosis of Type II diabetes. Now the pool and gym play a significant role by enabling me to maintain control without resorting to oral medication or insulin. We took the apartment immediately. The salesperson was astonished and said, "Are you sure you don't want to look at some others?" We had seen enough apartments to know this is what we wanted. Lois replied, "Absolutely not."

My grandfather was the only person I know of in my family who had diabetes. We were on the way driving home from a trip to Atlantic City when he stopped his car along Pulaski Highway because he was having difficulty seeing. My grandmother never learned to drive and I was too young. My father and mother came to get us. His physician immediately diagnosed diabetes.

How times have changed. Insulin was the only option then. Disposable insulin syringes were a thing of the future. Syringes and needles required boiling between each use to sterilize them. The needles, sharpened when dull, were not as fine as today's. Testing was almost primitive. Laboratory tests only provided the blood level at the time drawn. Urine testing was the only method possible at home. Since glucose should never be in the urine it only confirmed that blood sugar was uncontrolled. HA1C, the test that provides an average blood glucose level, was not available. Home blood glucose monitoring came later. The oral anti-diabetic drugs became available during the 1950's. He was able to take them and could stop using insulin.

I learned I had diabetes at about the same age as my grandfather did. It is much easier for me than it was for him. Home blood glucose monitoring is easy. Insulin and oral drugs are much improved. Disposable insulin syringes, when/if needed, eliminate sterilization and are virtually painless.

Diagnosis was a stroke of luck. I saw my internist for something minor. He suggested a physical since my last "annual" physical had been more than four years earlier. The following month I had the physical and learned I had Type II diabetes. Over two years have passed and I am still able to control by blood sugar through weight loss, exercise and diet. I dodged a bullet, at least for the time being.

Diabetes has no symptoms until it is rather far along. Had my doctor not brought up the issue of a physical it could have been a long time before I found I had diabetes. This unquestionably would have made it more difficult to control and to avoid complications. Lois has been a major factor in my success so far. She has a knack for reminding me without actually reminding me or telling me, I should do something. "If you are going to test before dinner, do it now," or, Are you going to the gym today?" are phrases she uses. Lois knows that I am less likely to do something if "ordered" to do it.

This is especially important for my children and grandchild. Danielle. Lois's paternal grandmother, mother and uncle all had diabetes. The genetic component, from both sides of the family, places my children and grandchildren at an increased risk. The risk increases with age. Maintaining a normal weight, exercise and limiting the amount of carbohydrate in your diet is prudent but does not eliminate the increased risk. It is important that you have a blood glucose test done periodically. Impaired glucose tolerance and pre-diabetes are not "technically" diabetes, but still cause blood vessel damage, and should be dealt with sooner rather than later. The earlier the diagnosis the sooner treatment can begin. The sooner blood sugar is under control the greater the risk reduction.

My son Gregory and Cheryl married in 1956. My granddaughter, Danielle, was born the following year.

My daughter Leslie and Loren were together for seventeen years when Loren was killed in an automobile accident. Not many days go by when I don't think about him. I can't imagine how difficult this has been for Leslie. I don't know how one deals with the death, especially an untimely one, of a spouse.

My granddaughter Danielle and Jason have been together since 2002. Lois and I got a ready-made great-grandson. Lucas, Jason's son from a previous marriage, was three years old at that time.

WORK—
A GOOD FOUR-LETTER WORD

"Neither look for nor expect gratitude but
rather gather whatever comfort you can
out of the belief that your effort
is constructive in purpose."
Winston Churchill

Much like my mother, I would rather work at a job than work around the house. My work ethics and my father's work ethics are very much alike. I cannot recall him ever missing a day because of snow. I did miss one. The plows clearing Hamilton Avenue blocked the two exits out of the development. The neighbors got shovels and cleared a lane to Hamilton Avenue. By then it was late afternoon and too late to get to work. My father was always on time. Being on time is imperative to me. If I am not fifteen minutes early for work, I feel I am late. My father regularly worked a second job. I never had more than one job at a time, but often stayed late or worked weekends. I never worked because I had to, but because I wanted to. On weekends or snowy days Lois would ask, "Do you really have to go in today?" My answer was usually, "No, but I want to." I enjoyed working. Lois thinks I was crazy. I was entitled to four weeks vacation at the School of Pharmacy. Each year I just took the time needed for the vacation we planned. I would rather be working than sitting around the house. I saw no reason to stay home just because I could. The only time I took my full four weeks vacation was the final four weeks before retiring from pharmacy school. Offered a position as manager of the outpatient pharmacy of a hospital I was at work before my vacation was up.

Regardless of where I was working or how much I liked what I was doing, I was always ready to try something new. I did what I liked and I liked what I did. When I stopped liking what I was doing, it was time to do something else.

My first business venture, selling flowers, was before I started first grade. I gathered flowers from my grandmother's garden, put them in a basket, added a For Sale sign (written for me) and put the basket on the sidewalk. Later that day I found ten cents in the basket and the flowers were gone. That was my first and only sale but it was the first step of becoming an entrepreneur. My guess is my grandmother took the flowers and left the money.

My first job real was in 1950 at Belmar Pharmacy, but not because of any particular interest in pharmacy. I just wanted a job. Dick Greaves, a friend who worked there, said they needed someone part time. Belmar Pharmacy was a typical independent community pharmacy in an era when pharmacy practice was changing. Pharmacists did a great deal of counter prescribing for minor illnesses and referring patients to physicians when appropriate. Typically, a pharmacist filled prescriptions unseen in a back room. The mystique was part of the therapy. A peephole allowed the pharmacist to keep an eye on the front. A clerk or pharmacist took the prescription from the patient and disappeared. Shortly the pharmacist would appear with a bottle of medicine. Patients rarely knew the name of their drug. The law prevented pharmacists from including the drug name on the label unless requested by the physician. The law requires the opposite today. Tubes of creams had their original labels removed and replaced with the prescription label. If the tube had a painted label pharmacists either transferred the contents to an ointment jar or used acetone to remove it. Given just the prescription bottle, a hospital or physician wanting to identify the drug had to call the pharmacy with the prescription number. Without the prescription number, it was impossible to locate the original prescription. If the pharmacy was not open, there was no way to identify the drug. Pharmacists never told a patient the name of a drug or its use. According to the school of pharmacy (at that time) the best way for a pharmacist to respond to, a "What is this for?" type of question was to ask why the person went to the doctor. Then use the response to create an answer. Other than antibiotics and insulin, very few drugs had expiration dates. There was no way to determine how old a bottle of medicine might be. Sublingual nitroglycerin was particularly vulnerable because it vaporizes and loses strength rapidly. A law requiring a prescription label to have an expiration date of no more than one year from the date of dispensing came much later. This all seems archaic now but that was the accepted way at the time.

    Carroll Foster, the owner of Belmar Pharmacy, lived above the store with his family. This was common then. I worked as a clerk, soda jerk, delivery boy and clean-up boy at the store. I started just a few weeks before I was sixteen. Letting a novice drive is not a good idea but Doc Foster let me. I began delivering as soon as a got my license. Fortunately, I never had an accident. We delivered ice cream sundaes as well as prescriptions and anything else sold in the store. One wintery evening I used my grandfather's car to get to the drugstore. It had snowed and there were patches of ice that were hard to see. On my way home, I stepped on the brakes, causing the car to spin around 360 degrees. One of the rear wheels hit the curb. I told my grandfather the damage occurred where I parked the car. I don't know why I said this, and I don't know if he believed me or not. He never said anything. There was no reason for me to fear telling him the truth. I regretted it soon after but could never bring myself to tell him the real story. He was so wonderful to me that I feel bad about this even today. This is the first anyone every heard this story.

    At that time, every community pharmacy had a soda fountain. Most pharmacists believed them to be essential. Belmar had a small soda fountain where I dipped ice cream and made milk shakes, sundaes, ice cream sodas and phosphates. Can you get phosphates anywhere now? There was no food served at the fountain. There were two round, marble top, wrought iron tables. Each table had four wire back chairs that completed the ambiance of an era that was beginning to disappear. A similar antique ice cream set is on our balcony at Briarcliff. Beneath the cash register counter was a stand that held three large rolls of white wrapping paper. On the counter was a dispenser of red twine. By tradition, everything possible left the store wrapped in white paper and tied with red string. It took a lot of practice to wrap several oddly shaped items together. Using a bag was the alternative, but only as a last resort.

Most stock was in showcases, behind the glass doors of wall shelves or in drawers behind the counter. At the tobacco counter were tobacco and film products. There were a few self-service shelves. Among them were those with feminine hygiene products. In keeping with the custom at that time, they were on shelves, but inside brown paper bags labeled "J," "R," or "S" in crayon. This was to avoid embarrassment. Since this was the only thing displayed in a bag, I do not think it fooled anyone. The condoms were out of sight in drawers.

Should someone request something I was unfamiliar with, I was told to as ask, "What is this used for?" This would provide a clue to where I would find it. One evening a woman requested Fibs (a tampon I had never heard of). "What is this used for?" I asked. The poor woman became flustered and did not know what to say. Doc Foster overheard the conversation and completed the sale. I don't know who was more embarrassed the woman or me.

I really enjoyed working at Belmar Pharmacy. I left, but do not remember why. It could have been more money, more hours or maybe just another, "it seemed like a good idea at the time" decision.

My next job was at Bell Drug, located on Belair Road across the street from the Overlea Diner. Bell Drug had everything that Belmar Pharmacy had but was much larger and had a greater variety of sundries. They also sold liquor and had a huge inventory of gifts. I made deliveries and worked at the soda fountain. The fountain also had booths and served food as well as fountain products. I sold many tuna salad sandwiches, BLT's, hot dogs, hamburgers and grilled cheese sandwiches. I made tuna fish salad and chicken salad. Cubed white bread, put into these salads, made it look as though you were getting more tuna or chicken. Drug was a teenage hangout for my friends from Kenwood High School. When they got ice cream, an extra dip went in the milk shake or soda. I filled a cone with Ice cream first, and then the one or two scoops ordered went on top. This was not a bad job but not nearly as nice an atmosphere as that at Belmar Pharmacy. So far, my pharmacy jobs had not provided any experience in the prescription department.

Maurice LeBrun, a friend since the fourth grade, told me he had just gotten a part time job at Woolworths for the Christmas holidays. He told me they were looking for an additional part time person. I applied and got the job. My main job was working in the stock room receiving merchandise, pricing individual items (no bar codes then), stocking the basement warehouse shelves and carrying stock to the appropriate counters upstairs. As Christmas neared both the number of shoppers and the number of shoplifters increased. I began wearing a suit and a tie, and became a floorwalker. I considered growing a moustache to appear more mature. However, I rejected the idea because it would take at least until Easter to grow. My job was to prevent shoplifting. Mostly, I just roamed around the store trying to look important. Lois stopped in now and then and we would talk. When known or suspected shoplifters came, I would follow them closely. I hope I prevented shoplifting because I never saw anyone try to steal anything on my watch. I stayed on after Christmas but Maurice did not. I am not sure whether he quit or was let go. This was a good job. Everyone was very friendly, easy to work with and made me feel like I was one of them.

Overlea Pharmacy, at Belair Road and Overlea Avenue, was

much like Belmar Pharmacy except a little smaller. I began working for the owner, Francis (Frank) Balassone, in 1952 just after I entered pharmacy school. Paul Freed, a friend from boy scouts, who was in dental school, also worked there. The staff consisted of just a pharmacist and a clerk. Prescriptions were filled in the back room. There was a peephole to keep and eye on the front. Even though I was a clerk, soda jerk and delivery boy, Frank gave me the opportunity to help fill prescriptions. He taught me a great deal about pharmacy and was a wonderful human being. I have fond memories of working there. His wife and children came into the pharmacy so I came to know them also. Frank truly cared about his patients. If a physician wrote "PP" (poor patient) at the top of a prescription, that patient received a discounted price. To avoid embarrassing them, Frank never told them about the special price.

One evening I worked with his relief pharmacist. When not busy out front I walked to the back to help fill prescriptions. He said I should, "Go out front where I belonged." I not only went out front, I went out the front door. The following afternoon on my way home from pharmacy school, I stopped at the pharmacy with some trepidation. Frank had every right to fire me for walking out on the relief man. I kept my job and never had to work with that relief man again. Two peculiarities come to mind when I think of Overlea Pharmacy. The first was the prescription room trashcan. There was a small trap door under the trashcan. The can had no bottom but sat over a hole in the floor. Pull a rope, the trap door opened, the trash fell through and went into a carton in the basement ready for trash collection. The second was the organization of the prescription stock. Pharmacies usually stock drugs in A to Z order to simplify locating them. The previous owner ran out of space, added more shelves and started the alphabet over. Overlea Pharmacy then had two separate A to Z systems. Frank never changed that so there were always two places to look for a drug.

Frank had a great interest in the pharmacy profession. Some years later, he gave up Overlea Pharmacy to become the Secretary of the

Maryland Board of Pharmacy and Chief of the Division of Drug Control. He was influential in facilitating the changes in the laws that were necessary to allow the School of Pharmacy to develop the Professional Experience Program (PEP). I eventually became the director of this program.

For three summers (1953, 54, 55) while in pharmacy school, I worked in the Union Memorial Hospital for the Director of Pharmacy, Mr. Morris. This was great experience. I actually practiced pharmacy and satisfied some of my experiential requirements for licensure examination during my summers here. For nine months of the year, the staff was Mr. Morris, another pharmacist (Gene) and a porter. I was there for the three summer months. Since Mr. Morris and Gene each had four weeks of vacation, this provided a real opportunity for me. Hospital pharmacy was far different then, from now. The pharmacy was not open nights or Sundays. A medicine needed after we closed came from Burris and Kemp Pharmacy. If Burris and Kemp could not supply it, the head nurse had access to the pharmacy to obtain the medicine. She would leave a note so that the pharmacy could bill the patient. It was not illegal at the time but is now. There were no fax machines or computers. Prescription orders were hand written and brought to the pharmacy. The container for tablets or capsules was a small paper envelope with the drug name, patient's name and room number typed on it. The tablets and capsules were in the envelopes loose because there was no unit dose packaging. We used glass bottles for liquids. Periodically, a porter from each floor would pick up the medicines. I compounded eye drops not available from manufacturers. Although we did the best we could using aseptic techniques, complete sterility was not possible. We didn't have a better way, but I now wonder how many problems resulted.

One of my regular tasks was to dilute 95% ethyl alcohol to 70% for back rubs. I added yellow coloring to discourage people from drinking it. It didn't. The rubbing alcohol disappeared at a rapid rate. Seventy percent alcohol makes a very stiff drink. The doctors and nurses said the porters drank it. It must have been them because we all know that doctors, nurses and pharmacists would never drink on the job. Who knows where it really went. Actually, I do know where some of this alcohol went at Christmas time. Mr. Morris was friendly with the chef. Actually, Mr. Morris was friendly with everybody. Periodically the chef provided us with sandwiches. We returned the favor at Christmas. The chef brought us oranges, we provided the alcohol and made a "holiday drink" for the staff.

Union Memorial Hospital was a good place to work. Working with the hospital staff was very pleasant. We had no patient/customers to deal with since we did not fill outpatient prescriptions. Unheard of in community pharmacy at the time, the pharmacy closed evenings, weekends, holidays and lunch hours.

In the 1950's the Post Office delivered mail several times a day for several weeks prior to Christmas. The Post Office hired temporary workers to supplement the regular carriers during this period. Each Christmas while I was in pharmacy school I worked at the Raspeburg sub-station. The job was ideal. I began after the last day of the semester and worked through Christmas Eve. All I did was deliver the mail. The regular carrier sorted and arranged the bags. Part way through the route, about the time my bag was empty, there would be another bagful left in a mailbox for me. The first time I came back for my second trip the regular carrier asked, "Why are you back so soon? What did you do, run?" I thought I had taken my time. Out there with no one watching, it would have been easy to goof off but I never did. I walked my normal pace but never rushed. Time seems to pass faster when doing something. The first day I ate my lunch at a small restaurant on Belair Road. I ordered pie for dessert. As I got up to leave, I saw the dish dusted off with a towel and put away unwashed. I never ate there again. I don't recall there being anyone else in the restaurant. Maybe there was a reason. A smarter person would at least wait until after I left.

My senior year at pharmacy school I began working part-time with the Read Drug and Chemical Company. Reads was the only chain pharmacy of consequence in Baltimore. In 1956, pharmacists were in short supply. Read's pharmacists often had to wait until a recent graduate received a license before he (there were almost no female pharmacists at that time) could take a vacation. To try to relieve this situation, Reads hired pharmacy students and paid them well. The expectation was that the pay and a ready-made position upon licensure would keep them there after graduation.

I took the pharmacy licensure examination the summer following my graduation (1956) from the University Of Maryland School Of Pharmacy. Candidates learned of their successful completion of the examination through an announcement placed in the newspaper. That November my name was included (mistakenly, I learned later) among those of the newly licensed pharmacists.

Read's immediately transferred me to the Middlesex Shopping Center store as the assistant manager and the only pharmacist. Now I was a real pharmacist, or so I thought. Every January Reads reported the license numbers of every pharmacist they employed to the Maryland Board of Pharmacy. Since I never bothered to pick up my license, I had no idea what the number was. I called the Board of Pharmacy and learned that they disallowed half of my internship hours from Union Memorial Hospital because, "it was only hospital pharmacy." My name in the newspaper was their mistake, but I still had internship hours to complete. By this time I had been working alone as a pharmacist for about three months. By some twisted logic of a board dominated by community pharmacists, those who worked in retail pharmacies got full credit for all their hours, often at cigar/cigarette counters, soda fountains, delivering, etc. I, on the other hand, only got half credit while doing nothing but pharmacy. Since there was no other pharmacist at Middlesex, the board decided to allow me to document my own experience. I did and received my license. I was officially and legally a pharmacist as of February 15, 1957. That fall Reads promoted me to manager and assigned me to the North Point

Village store. The promotion entitled me to the usual $ 0.05 per hour raise. Now I was making $2.00 an hour. That may not sound like much but I had saved enough for the down payment on a new car before the end of the year. In addition, there would be a bonus at the end of the year based upon the store's performance. The pharmacist was responsible for the overall management of the entire store so I gained a lot of valuable experience while at Read's.

Bernard, Marvin and Leona

Kenny and Me

Garage, Gas Pump and Car

First Day at Elementary School

Ready to Dance

High School Graduation

Private, Maryland National Guard

Parents and Grandparents Visit Jamboree

St. James Evangelical Lutheran Church

Lois, Beautiful in White

Deep Creek Lake, Maryland

Grandmother and Mother
(1915)

Philip Dannenfelser, Sr. and Philip Dannenfelser, Jr.

ATLANTIC CITY, A DIAMOND RING AND PHARMACY OWNERSHIP

In 1959, while working for Reads, Lois and I took a vacation to Atlantic City. It was a beach town then, not a gambling town. Harry and Edna kept Gregory and Leslie. It began to rain while we were walking the boardwalk so we ducked into an auction house to wait for the weather to clear. Sometimes bidding would stop at less that the amount the auctioneer anticipated. To stimulate more bidding he would go through the audience asking, "Would you give me $100.00 (or whatever the last bid was) for this?" Everyone answered "Yes" because there was no obligation; someone else had already bid this amount. The intent was just to get people talking. He was auctioning off a diamond ring and had a bid for $135.00. Then he added a watch, looked at Lois and asked, "Would you give me $150.00 for the watch and this ring?" Not realizing the slight change in the words, Lois said, "Yes." The auctioneer said, "Sold!" I am not sure who was more surprised, Lois or me. I went to the desk to complete the transaction. Later I found out Lois had no interest in the ring but thought she was doing what the others had done before. I did not have $150.00; I had less than $50.00. I gave them most of the money I had as a deposit. They were to send the watch and ring when they received the balance. We arrived home with less than $5.00. What a dilemma! Would sending a check be throwing good money after bad? Would they actually send me the watch and ring? Was it even worth what I paid? I decided to send them the money. Shortly thereafter, the watch and ring came in the mail. Unsure of the value of my purchase I took the ring to a jewelry store for an appraisal. No sooner was the ring out of my pocket when the jeweler said, "Where did you get this, Atlantic City?" My heart sank. Now I was certain that buying this was a mistake. The jeweler valued the ring at $150.00 and charged me $15.00 for the appraisal. He also said there was nothing wrong with the ring. He recognized as the style of ring made especially for the Atlantic City auctions. I think I was lucky to come out as well as I did.

Not too long after the appraisal, Lois and I visited Tedd while he was working at Rutkowski's Pharmacy. We related the ring story. He said he always wanted his mother to have a diamond ring and paid us $150.00 for it. Harry paid us $15.00 for the watch and gave it to Carole for a birthday present. We ended up breaking even and having a good story to tell. Carole inherited the ring after Tedd's mother died so it remains in the family.

There is a lesson here, "Be extra careful at auctions." However, I never learned it. Years later The Hunt Valley Marriott held periodic auctions of items from estates, repossessions, etc. Lois and I would look over what they had on display and occasionally buy something. One Sunday a rack displayed fur coats. Lois tried several on. I asked her if she liked one I thought was spectacular. She said, "Yes." When this full length, white mink coat bordered in white fox came up, I got the bid. It was then that Lois said, "I hope it fits." Hope it fits! The ring in Atlantic City was bad enough but this! She had the coat on but never thought about the coat fitting because she did not think I would bid on it. It did fit and she has enjoyed wearing it every winter since. This did teach me a lesson. At future auctions, we looked at all the items on display, chose those that interested us and decided on our maximum bid. There has been no more auction confusion since.

Like many of my classmates, I was on the lookout for the opportunity to become a pharmacy owner. My time with Reads was enjoyable but I periodically looked at pharmacies offered for sale.

MEMOIRS AND MORE

Should an opportunity arise, I was prepared to resign. Tedd Pruss, a classmate and friend from pharmacy school continued on to the pharmacology graduate there. He temporarily dropped out in order to manage Rutkowski's Pharmacy for his aunt after his uncle died. In 1958, Tedd asked if I was interested in managing the pharmacy for his aunt when he went back to graduate school. I said I would, but only if I had an option to buy. Dorothy Rutkowski and I came to an agreement. I resigned from Reads. This was before the year ended so I never received a manager's bonus. My objective of ownership was coming closer.

The pharmacy was established about 1905 as Grau's Pharmacy. Edward and Dorothy Rutkowski purchased the pharmacy from the son of the original owner and changed the name to Rutkowski's Pharmacy. Little in the pharmacy had changed since 1905. I remodeled and modernized it. The marble cabinet and mirror was the back bar of the original soda fountain. It is now in our dining room along with the pharmacy balances.

Rutkowski's was a typical neighborhood pharmacy of that time. I have fond memories of working in Highlandtown. Most of the customers were neighbors who if not personal friends were very friendly. I knew almost every customer by name. Everyone called me Doc. Customers brought cookies or other baked goods and sent cards at Christmas. This was an era when many people often consulted a community pharmacist before seeing a physician. There were always questions about childhood diseases (measles, mumps and chicken pox) as well as a lot of counter prescribing for colds and other minor illnesses. People came into check if a symptom needed a physician's attention. I removed splinters, took things out of peoples' eyes and bandaged cuts. Highlandtown was not a wealthy area but the people were frugal and nearly always paid cash. A returned check was a rarity. During my entire time there, only one returned check was never made good. I did not accept credit cards because I never had anyone request to use one. Charges were unusual. Those that did usually paid without my sending a bill. My accounts receivable system was a file box with about a dozen index cards. Most had zero balances. There was one customer who always carried a balance. It was never very high but he never completely paid it off. I came to know him well. He did some painting for me at home and helped me out of a jam when I needed someone who could drive a tractor-trailer truck.

I am not the brilliant innovator who develops new concepts. However, I do recognize when and how to adopt and adapt ideas to enhance a business. Before pharmacy computers became available, relatively few pharmacists maintained patient profiles because it was labor intensive and impractical for much beyond providing a list of the patient's prescriptions and prescription numbers. I was one of those few. One year, as a marketing strategy to enhance good will, I totaled each patient's prescription expenses from the profiles and mailed them the amount for income tax purposes. I spent many evenings after work adding, transferring the total to a preprinted form, addressing envelopes and mailing one to every family. Talk about labor intensive! After this, I only provided them when requested.

The next step was to design a label format to make it possible to type the label, receipt and profile information simultaneously. The new format was more efficient and the information was more useful. The label section is affixed to the prescription container and the profile portion is affixed to a family profile form. The complete records for an entire family were now in one place. All the information needed to process a refill was on the profile. This eliminated the need to retrieve the original prescription, saving a significant amount of time.

Pharmacy computer systems changed everything. I recognized that a pharmacy computer would very likely change pharmacy practice dramatically and began researching the possibilities. There were probably less than a dozen or two pharmacies in Baltimore when I installed my first computer. The early computer systems collected data and increased efficiency but added nothing new. A large amount of data was collected but was not useable. There was a realization that this information, when manipulated, could provide numerous useful services. In a relative few years, it became impossible to operate a pharmacy without a computer.

There is no division of labor in the management of a small pharmacy. The owner wears all the hats. It may involve more work but I do not mind that. In fact, I prefer it. I want to be in charge and I want to make the decisions. If there is a right way, a wrong way and my way, I want things done my way. On the one hand, I can take credit for what goes right. On the other, I have to assume responsibility for what goes wrong. That is what makes the job a challenge. That is what makes management and ownership satisfying. That is what makes work enjoyable.

Rutkowski's Pharmacy did not have a soda fountain but did sell packaged ice cream. I spoke with a sales representative from the Hershey Ice Cream company. He told me I could sell Hershey Ice cream for ten cents per half gallon less than the Delvale Ice Cream I currently sold. I liked the idea of the Hershey brand name as much as the lower selling price. Hershey delivered a new freezer, stocked it and took my remaining ice cream and the old freezer back to Delvale. The next day I checked the invoice and saw that my cost from Hershey was identical to what I was paying Delvale. I was just selling it for less! I would have gladly paid Hershey that price. However, I trust people but despise being misled. I called Hershey and told them I was misled and to come pick up their ice cream and freezer.

I am trustworthy and expect others to be. We sold money orders to our customers who did not have checking accounts. The fee for a money order was split between the pharmacy and the money order company. Each week I sent a check, less our commission to the money order company. Now and then, I would receive a notice that I had miscalculated and underpaid them. I re-checked, found they were right, and sent them the difference. At some point, a light went on. I never received a notice that I overpaid them. Had I never make a mistake in their favor? Intentionally, I sent ten dollars too much. The following week, I sent ten dollars too little. Then I waited. A bill for the ten dollars I shorted them arrived. I waited several more weeks but never heard anything regarding the extra ten dollars I sent. I contacted them and told them why I would no longer do business with them any longer. The response was, "You would have gotten the $10.00 sooner or later." That did not satisfy me.

In 1963, after three years in partnership with Dorothy Rutkowski, I purchased her interest and changed the name to Marvin Oed Pharmacy. This pharmacy had an inordinate number of unusual customers for a small store. There was a man who came every Friday morning, used our pay phone and then went into a house across the street. I cannot really call him a customer because he never once bought anything. One morning I noticed what appeared to be a gift under a folded newspaper. My assumption was that the woman across the street was his girl friend and he was taking her a gift. The woman was married so my next assumption was that the phone call was to make certain the husband was at work before he went in. This went on for many months and remained a mystery.

Another regular customer was very pleasant and appeared quite normal for a long time. No one questioned why he bought two-ounce prescription bottles periodically. We sold one now and then, but he was the only person who got them regularly. One afternoon, I overheard him say to the clerk, Marge Kirmse, "You won't believe what I want these for." Of course, that prompted the question, "What do you want them for?" It seems he puts liquor in them for his brother. What made it unusual is that the liquor was for his brother who died several years earlier but still liked to drink. He was right about one thing. I did not believe him. From then on, we heard stories on a regular basis. Angels visited him because they liked the beds at his house. Mother Teresa stopped in on her way to Rome when her wings iced up. A saint, very tall and with a long white beard, wanted Prell Shampoo to wash his hair. The one I like best is that the pint of ice cream he bought was for Jesus wanted it to soothe his sore throat.

A third man was deathly afraid of germs. However, he continually did things that then caused him great, although unwarranted, concern. He might take up to twenty minutes seeking assurance that he was not about to come down with some dread disease because of something he had just done or touched. Eventually it would appear I alleviated his fears. He would start to leave, but the closer he got to the exit the slower he walked. Then he would turn around, come back to me and repeat the same concerns all over again. This might be repeated three or four times. Each time he came in it was a different problem. After he stepped on a sewer grate, he was afraid of getting bubonic plague from the rats that were likely to be in the sewer. Another time it was touching broken glass in a graveyard. I will attempt to word the next one delicately. He said me he paid a 'lady' for certain 'services' and described one involving his mouth contacting a part of her upper torso. Because of her occupation, he feared germs from another customer were transmitted to him. Finally, I had a solution for a problem for him. I sold him a bottle of Listerine mouthwash. After getting his hat back from having it cleaned and blocked, (I did not know people still did that) he was alarmed because the cleaner had stuffed his hat with bathroom tissue. A relief pharmacist, Jim Edelen, liked to make a game out of dealing with him. One morning he came to Jim. He had just been to a number of stores and was afraid he had germs on his hands from the doorknobs and that he transferred those germs from one store to another. Jim gave him a bottle of alcohol and some paper towels. He told him to go back to the stores he had visited to wipe all the door handles with the alcohol. Did anyone notice this man walking store-to-store and wiping doorknobs with alcohol? Did they wonder why?

A fourth man periodically got mad at God. I could see and hear him a block away waving his fist and yelling at Sacred Heart Church. When he came into the pharmacy he was pleasant, but usually disheveled and in need of a bath and a shave. Most often, he just related some story that made no sense at all. He regularly visited funeral homes and brought me the memorial cards he picked up there.

What did the mourners think when this scruffy looking man they did not know visited their deceased loved one? He lived with his mother a few blocks from the store. One day he told me that his mother fell off the sofa and would not get up. I did not know whether this was real or fantasy. Afraid that something could be wrong, I called the police. An hour or two later the police came back and said the odor coming from the house was so bad they could smell the stench from the sidewalk. They found her on the floor, her leg gangrenous and covered with maggots. They called for paramedics. The ambulance took her to the hospital. I am so glad that I did not ignore him. Who knows what would have happened?

A regular customer began walking to work because he did not have the $150.00 he needed to get his car fixed. A day or two later he said the way out of his predicament was to but a new car. He read and ad in the newspaper that Luby's Chevrolet would take "any car" as the down payment for a new one. I asked how he expected to make the monthly payments on a new car if he was unable to pay $150.00 to fix the old one. He did not have an answer and I never learned how or if he came up with the money. The same customer bought a side of beef in a deal that included the rental of a freezer. His family ate all the meat but he still had several months left on the freezer rental.

Strange people were not limited to customers. On a day off, I was in the stockroom of the store building some shelves. My relief pharmacist walked back and said he was quitting. He gave no reason other than, "I have to leave." I asked how much notice he was giving me. His answer was, "I'm leaving now." He left with a patient waiting and a label, half-typed, in the typewriter. I filled prescriptions the rest of the day in work clothes. I never had any indication of a problem but later learned he was an alcoholic.

The female graduate student I hired to replace him ate pickles while working. Every morning after she worked the prescription counter was sticky with pickle juice. I learned that the lab coat she wore was always dirty. It was unbuttoned, she said, "Because it made it easier to reach the higher shelves." That also made it easier to see her dirty underwear. One evening she left the clerk in the store alone and met her boyfriend for dinner. That was her last day working for me.

I was always ready to consider something new. About 1970, after expanding into hospital equipment, the name changed to Marvin Oed Pharmacy and Medical Equipment. Later the pharmacy and medical equipment became two separate businesses.

Spectro Industries, the parent company of our local drug wholesaler, was developing Medical Equipment Unlimited (MEU) agencies. Pharmacists buying this franchise-like agency received training to fit braces and to sell and/or rent a wide variety of medical supplies and equipment. I saw this as an opportunity to expand into an entirely new area and purchased an agency, completed the training, installed a fitting room and rented a garage for storage. Two people were added to handle the medical equipment aspect of the business. My son Gregory completed the training courses. He fit braces, sold and rented equipment, made sales calls and assisted the deliveryman when necessary.

Our initial marketing attempts were health screenings in the pharmacy. One of the first things Gregory did was conduct a blood pressure screening. Although commonplace now they were relatively unusual at that time.

It was not long before sales, rentals, and brace fittings left insufficient time for marketing, which limited our growth. At first, I became my own sales representative. What was I thinking? I should have known better. It was not that I did not like selling. I loathed selling. When I approached an office door, I hoped no one would be there.

I was treating medical equipment as a department within the pharmacy. That was wrong. The medical equipment and orthotics businesses are very different from the pharmacy business. We expanded into respiratory care and created Marvin Oed Medical

Equipment as a separate entity. To finance the expansion required a second mortgage. That concerned Lois but I was not aware of it at the time. There may have been indications but she never said anything until this year (2008). I never notice nuances, if you expect me to know something, be direct.

Gregory was learning the business but we needed immediate help. I hired David Smoller as a salesman and brace fitter. He and Gregory worked together as they both learned the business. Eventually Gregory had full responsibility for managing Marvin Oed Medical Equipment.

The staff consisted of Gregory, Dave Smoller, two deliverymen, a respiratory therapist, and an office coordinator. My daughter Leslie was an office assistant. The office coordinator had the responsibility of obtaining the required physician and patient information, scheduling deliveries and pickups and billing Medicare. For a time Lois and my sister-in-law, Janice Scheler shared the job of office coordinator.

The level of service provided to their agencies by Medical Equipment Unlimited never lived up to expectations. The promotional sales calls promised never happened, backup support was poor and the equipment inventory was inadequate. Dave and I pointed this out several times to them in telephone calls and letters. Nothing improved. In 1974, Spectro asked if we thought we could do it better. Our answer was yes. We made an agreement with Spectro Industries and formed a new company, Medical Equipment Unlimited of Maryland, Inc.

We did improve those things we had control over. We sold additional agencies and provided the backup support. Gregory and I participated in the educational programs. However, we had no control over one major problem, the wholesaler's inadequate inventory. That never improved. The successful agencies began purchasing elsewhere. Because we were paid based on wholesaler sales, our income was limited. Promoting our own business would be more productive. We parted with MEU and Spectro amicably in 1976.

Dave eventually left. I believe he had hopes of eventually

becoming a partner or owner of the business and realized that with Gregory there that was unlikely. We parted on friendly terms. Dave was an excellent salesman, very aggressive and at 5'6" and 485 pounds, unforgettable. I replaced him with his exact opposite. Jerry Lotz was also an excellent salesman but was laid back, methodical, conscientious and reliable—just an all around nice guy. Jerry was good enough that Phil Levin from Spectro asked if he could talk to Jerry about a position with them. (This was a time when more people were honorable.) Of course, I said yes. Jerry was much too nice to just say, "I quit." He was unaware that I knew about the offer and had a difficult time telling me. The offer he had was more than I could afford and I told him so. I told him that the right thing for any employee to do is what is best for him and his family. In addition, I said that I would rather have him working for me but that this seemed to be a real opportunity for him. As much as I hated to lose him, I felt good that working for me led to something better for him. We remain friendly and still hear from him.

While working together Gregory and I learned of a company called Medicare Data Services (MDS). The majority of people requesting medical equipment qualify for Medicare. The Medicare rules and regulations were (are?) so complex that they make it difficult for patients, physicians and providers to comply. Therefore, most equipment providers did not accept Medicare assignment. Typically, providers collected from the patient and gave them a completed Medicare form. Unless completely and accurately filled out, the patient was left with the most complex and confusing task of trying to obtain reimbursement from Medicare. It was common that patients with legitimate requests for reimbursement to be denied. Challenging a denial was often a long, laborious, and often unsuccessful, process. Medicare Data Services (MDS) developed a system for systematically managing medical equipment rentals through Medicare. Their system would enable Marvin Oed Medical Equipment to provide equipment immediately assurance that payment would be forthcoming. Recognizing the potential marketing advantage of such a program Gregory and I completed MDS training and implemented their systems.

With just a few telephone calls, we accepted Medicare assignments and delivered equipment immediately. This was a win win situation for everyone involved. Discharge planners were happy because we saved them time and relieved them of a complex task. Physicians were happy because we provided exactly what they needed to justify a claim. Patients were happy because they got the equipment without having to deal with prepaying and waiting for Medicare reimbursement. We were happy because the system provided us with an excellent marketing tool and assured, virtually, of payment. MDS also provided computerized Medicare claims processing that greatly reduced the volume of our paperwork. We later purchased a system and processed our own bills. This system, uncommon then, which enabled us to build our rental business, is now commonplace.

In 1969, a pharmacy journal ran an article about a pharmacy franchise, Medicine Shoppe International (MSI). Their concept was a professional pharmacy that provided prescriptions at competitive prices. Medicine Shoppes opened eight hours daily, half a day on Saturday and closed nights, Sundays and holidays. Marvin Oed Pharmacy, like most community pharmacies, was open nearly double that. This sounded like semi-retirement to me. I made an appointment. Lois and I flew to MSI headquarters in St. Louis. Ostensibly, this was to discuss converting Marvin Oed Pharmacy into a Medicine Shoppe. My intent was to see what they were doing and if I could apply some of their ideas in my operation. We met a vice president of MSI and spent an hour or two in a lounge at the St. Louis airport. His conclusion was that, given the current level of volume and earnings, converting to a Medicine Shoppe would mean a step back for a year or two. He said, "I can't recommend the conversion." Then he added, "Since you've come all the way here would you like to visit some of our stores before going home?" This may be the most subtle sales pitch ever. We visited several shoppes and discussed MSI's operational details allowing me to learn a lot more about their concepts. Everything made sense. The systems provided operational systems and controls that made them ideal as a second store. Lois and I flew home and a deposit went in the mail the next day. I was on my way to a second business.

MSI's emphasis was on marketing and promotion. I had access to individuals with business expertise that I lacked. They changed my thinking about management and marketing which enhanced my business skills in general. One of the most important lessons was always to ask the following three questions before making a decision. "Why do I want to do this?" Will this actually result in what I want?" "Is there another method that may be more effective or less expensive?" By combining a price guarantee and a pricing strategy that was a blend of science and art, we became competitive with the chain pharmacies. MSI showed me that "press releases" to local newspapers could become free advertisement in disguise. The *"Dundalk Eagle"* printed every article I submitted to them word for word.

MSI identified and analyzed potential sites. I visited each and we would discuss those that interested me. In 1970, MSI and I agreed on the 40 Dundalk Avenue location. I especially liked it because it was relatively convenient to both Marvin Oed Pharmacy in Highlandtown and my home in Rosedale. This turned out to be an excellent choice.

A manager of the Dundalk Avenue Medicine Shoppe (I'll call him Bill) and I went to St. Louis for a week for their training program. The shoppe began growing rapidly and then slowed. MSI's analysis was that that we had adequate staff to service our customers but at the expense of promotional efforts and recommended hiring additional staff. Once we did growth resumed. Another lesson learned. My first thought when MSI announced plans for health care screenings was, "What's the bid deal, I've already done that." There was a huge difference. They added a process that enabled us to encourage current customers to refer friends, identify potential new customers and get them to return to the shoppe. Another lesson learned. We screened for high blood pressure, diabetes, glaucoma, sickle cell, foot care, etc. The number of people attracted varied from just one to over four hundred. The four hundred was a diabetes screening. The day of the sickle cell screening not one person had shown up by 2:00pm. I was disappointed, to say the least. About 2:30pm, the only person to come that day arrived. As luck would have it, a TV camera crew showed up a few minutes later. Our sickle cell screening made the evening news. My disappointment changed to elation. What appeared to be our least successful screening may have been one of our most successful from a media marketing perspective. We converted many of those attending screenings into customers. The health screenings and personal presentations to senior groups became our most effective marketing tools.

"Bill" developed some personal problems that made it necessary to let him go. I hired a second manager, (I'll call him Bob). This worked well until "Bob" developed some personal problems also. The store opened 9:30 to 1:30 on Saturday. One Saturday at 10:00am, no one answered the shoppe when my wife Lois telephoned. Shortly thereafter, Lois called again and was told by someone (not an employee) that "Bill" was too busy to talk to her. Lois called me. I was there at closing time to talk with "Bill" about the late opening and a non-employee answering the telephone. He said he had some place to go and couldn't talk with me. I said, "If you walk out the door don't bother coming back." "Bill" left and was replaced by "Barry."

"Barry" completed the MSI training and did a good job as manager. About five years later, "Barry" began indicating an interest is becoming a pharmacy owner. Another pharmacy, on Wise Avenue in Dundalk, was for sale through a bankruptcy court. Although leery of partnerships, rather than lose "Barry" completely, I suggested we form a partnership, buy that pharmacy and convert it into a Medicine Shoppe. He would have full management responsibility. Regardless of how much or how little the pharmacy made, half of it would be mine. How could I lose? (I found out later.) I hired Frank Scholtz as the new manager. Frank was an excellent manager and stayed until I sold the Medicine Shoppe.

In 1980, "Barry" and I chose a corporate name that combine our wives names and re-opened the pharmacy on Wise Avenue as a Medicine Shoppe. This was a full line pharmacy so the inventory was inconsistent with the Medicine Shoppe format. Interestingly, we liquidated the incompatible inventory for more than we paid for the entire business, essentially showing a profit before we opened.

Since this originally was a large, full line pharmacy there was much more space than a Medicine Shoppe required. Medical equipment was in need of more room and utilized the extra space. "Barry" was responsible for the pharmacy operations. By now, Gregory had full responsibility for running Marvin Oed Medical Equipment.

The growth rate of the Medicine Shoppe was about as we expected initially but then leveled off. I assumed (a big mistake) an intensive promotional campaign promoting prescription co-pay discounts begun by several chain pharmacies was responsible. That was not it. "Barry" had a drug problem, left the partnership and went into treatment.

Operating statements are only useful when the information is accurate. The information "Barry" provided the accountants was not. The store had a severe financial problem that was not evident in the statements I received. I trusted him, gave him full responsibility and never interfered. Perhaps this could have turned out differently. Trust does not always pay, but it has always been, and still is, my style. "Always trust but always verify," is a business saying that I will not accept. If verification is necessary, trust does not exist. I would never enter a partnership if I thought I had to verify. This experience cost me money but it has not altered my attitude to trust everyone until he proves himself untrustworthy.

The pharmacy's sales volume was reported accurately, however our accounts payable were greatly understated. The past due payables were omitted from the reports. The cash was not available and I had neither the desire nor the will necessary to resolve the financial problems. It was time to get out.

To keep the pharmacy open until it sold, I hired a graduate student from pharmacy school to work for the summer. Just before he was to begin, a pharmaceutical manufacturer offered him a summer position that was too good to pass up. Now I was without a pharmacist. I immediately ruled out working the store myself and decided there were two options. One was to seek another pharmacist and continue trying to sell the store. The other was to just close the store and walk away. The payables were the major problem. If I hired a pharmacist and sold the store, the best I could expect was to be able to pay most, but probably not all, of our creditors. If the pharmacy closed, only one company could be paid. Either way I ended up with nothing. That ended it for me. I'd had enough. Medicine Shoppe International was aware of what was taking place. The following week I telephoned Ron Hofmeister, a V.P and friend at MSI. The conversation was short. After explaining what happened, I said, "When I lock the door on Saturday, I am not coming back. MSI can have the shoppe if they want it." MSI took over the following week. MSI asked if it was okay for "Bob" to manage the store for them since I had let him go. It was thoughtful of MSI to ask. It was their store and they could do whatever they wanted. This was a company and a time when people did not do things just because they could.

The inventory was sufficient to satisfy Loewy Drug Company, the only secured creditor. The others were large drug manufacturers (e.g., Parke-Davis). Writing off my debt would not be significant to them. I never reneged on a debt before and it still bothers me that unpaid bills remained. I have that gene from my father.

For a time I was teaching at the school of pharmacy while working or managing Marvin Oed Pharmacy, Marvin Oed Medical Equipment and the Dundalk Medicine Shoppe. There were several break-ins and attempted break-ins at the Marvin Oed Pharmacy. Although aggravating, the burglar alarms prevented any financial loss.

Three armed robberies are a different story. Fortunately, no one was ever injured. Anyone can reach the point where enough is enough. This was it for me. During the first robbery, a lone man robbed my mother, who was filling in for a clerk, and pharmacist Frank Cwynar. My mother took her experience surprisingly well. Two men came in each time for the second and third armed robberies. Each time I was there, once with Marge Kirmse, a clerk and the other with my daughter Leslie. My major concern during the first was one of the children living upstairs would come down for ice cream and interrupt the robbery. Based on their demeanor, I felt confident that if they got what they wanted they would leave. However, who knows what they would do if surprised. I gave them the drugs and they left. I was able to identify both from mug shots. Boy was my judgment about them wrong. I learned from the police that in two earlier robberies the same two stabbed one victim and shot and paralyzed the other. Neither had resisted. For weeks after, I was nervous whenever someone entered the store that I did not recognize. Later both were caught, went to trial and to jail. On a Saturday afternoon, two men came in when Leslie was working with me. One threatened her while the other came behind the prescription counter. He asked for drugs. I was more than willing to give them to him. The narcotics were in a locked cabinet but the keys were in the burglar alarm. This bothered him considerably. He made it clear that I was a dead man if the alarm went off when I took the keys out. It didn't, he got the drugs and they left. We were lucky three times, however, working in the pharmacy would never be the same.

I was always in the wrong place at the wrong time trying to juggle four jobs. Gregory managed the medical equipment while Pharmacy School and the Medicine Shoppe provided enough for me to do. I transferred the pharmacy inventory to the Medicine Shoppe and sold the prescription files to Highland Pharmacy. I am not sure why I chose not to sell the pharmacy. Maybe the business was so personal to me that I did not want to disclose anything to anyone. Perhaps it was that I just wanted to get out immediately. Financially, selling the business would have been a better alternative for me. It would also have been better for Dorothy Rutkowski who still owned the building. Dorothy had been good to me for a number of years. I closed the pharmacy without discussing it with her. Just because one has the right to do something, does not mean it is the right thing to do. The right way may have been the better for both of us. Dorothy was able to rent the space to another medical equipment company.

RETURN TO THE UNIVERSITY OF MARYLAND SCHOOL OF PHARMACY

Following my graduation, I had little contact with the School of Pharmacy until learning about the Professional Experience Program (PEP). A sales representative said I could get "free help" from students from the school. I was skeptical. If something seems too good to be true, it usually is. It did seem worth looking into. A structured, school supervised, externship program to replace the unstructured, unsupervised, post-graduation work experience requirement for pharmacy licensure examination was in its experimental stages. The school assigned each student to a series of pharmacist preceptors for training. The students were to learn the practice of pharmacy from practitioners. They were not "free help" because they could not replace an employee. Whatever tasks a student relieved me of was more than offset by the time taken to discuss, supervise, explain and evaluate. I enjoyed working with the students even though training took a substantial amount of time. To teach them I looked much more closely at the way I practiced. Therefore, I also learned. We tend to do things a certain way because they have always been done that way. Often outsiders see things overlooked by the person who sees it every day. My first student, Tony Tommasello, asked me why all the bottles containing infrequently used powders for compounding were on shelves at my fingertips. They were there when I came, and had probably been there since the pharmacy opened some sixty-five years earlier. I put the powders in the back room and used the space for frequently used items. After that, I tried to examine whatever I was doing and ask myself, "Is there a better way?"

Preceptor meetings at the school furthered my interest in the Professional Experience Program. The University of Maryland was the leader in the development of these programs and frequently had visitors from schools across the country. They wanted program details but also wanted to hear a preceptor's point of view. I spoke to them on several occasions. I liked telling students how and why I practiced pharmacy and I liked telling visiting professors how students benefited from practitioners teaching them the practice of pharmacy. I also began to assist in the Pharmacy Practice Laboratory and give lectures related to medical equipment and orthotics.

Apparently, my volunteer work at the School of Pharmacy and the interest I demonstrated in the Professional Experience Program caught someone's attention. Dr. Ralph Shangraw and Dr. Peter Lamy asked me to meet with them. Bill Edmondson, the Director of the Professional Experience Program, was leaving. I accepted an offer of a faculty appointment and assumed Bill Edmondson's position.

In addition to directing the Professional Experience Program, I continued to lecture in several management and practice related courses. When Henry Seidman died, I temporarily assumed responsibility for the pharmacy practice laboratory. It was apparent to me that pharmacy computers were to become the thing of the future. I already installed one in the Medicine Shoppe. It was easy to convince my computer provider that providing one for students in the practice laboratory was in his interest. Practice usually precedes education. This reversed that. The practice laboratory was now ahead of most pharmacies. Our students were learning to use a new technology that most practicing pharmacists were just considering.

I was in school in the 1950's when most students viewed pharmacy as a business. Now most view it as a profession. The truth is that it is a combination. One cannot exist without the other. The pharmacy curriculum offered some basic management courses but nothing that addressed the overall operation of a pharmacy. To help meet this perceived need, I developed and taught a course that required the students to write a business plan for opening a new or expanding an existing pharmacy. I chose this format because it required the students to consider both the operational and professional aspects of pharmacy. My personal experiences and utilizing Senior Corp of Retired Executives (SCORE) volunteers who had "been there and done that" added credibility to the course. Writing, neglected by our educational system for years, is a weakness in many students. A Towson University professor described methods that enhanced the students business writing skills. I learned quite a bit from him also.

During the fall semester, each faculty member is required to submit a list of goals for the coming academic year and report on the progress made toward accomplishing the goals set the previous year. Things changed during the ensuing year that often made the goals irrelevant. Other tasks would take priority as new needs arose. The dean or department chair assigned tasks, or I decided to attempt a new or cancel an old project. I never heard anything related to these reports. My guess is that they were a university or state requirement and it passed up the line with no one ever reading it. Since it seemed to be a waste of time and effort, I began listing only those objectives I knew I was certain to accomplish. This made my year-end report very easy. All I did was list every goal as completed.

Coming from using my "it seems like a good idea" style of running my businesses, I expected to learn a lot from this large organization. I did learn some things. I learned too many layers of management, too many systems, too many committees, too much over-sight; too many reports and a committee meeting for virtually everything often bog down an organization. The hierarchy of the school bewildered and bemused me. Committees do everything. Therefore, no individual is ever responsible for anything. I am still not certain whether this is a case of no one being in charge or everyone being in charge. My, "It seems like a good idea" style worked just as well and was much more efficient. Things would be different if a university had to run efficiently enough to show a profit.

Pharmacy school provided me with an opportunity for experiences I would never have otherwise. My CV includes Contributing Editor to *"U.S. Pharmacist,"* Editorial Consultant to *"Pharmacy Focus"* and author or co-author of sixteen articles in pharmacy journals. Research opportunities are limited for those who lack a doctoral degree but I participated in eight and was the principal investigator in one. I was an "expert witness" in several legal cases. It was not long that, although the cases were interesting and the money was good it, I realized it was not something I wanted to be a part of.

Frank Balassone, my employer at Overlea Pharmacy, became the Secretary of the Maryland Board of Pharmacy. He was instrumental in seeing that the Maryland Board of Pharmacy accepted the concept of a pharmacy school supervised experiential training. The University of Maryland at Baltimore School of Pharmacy became the first school in the United States to graduate students who met all their experiential requirements for licensure examination within a school curriculum. The Professional Experience Program (PEP) became a model for similar programs throughout the USA. It pleases me that I was an integral part of its development and expansion.

I wanted to express the schools appreciation to the pharmacists who were the first preceptors and critical to the development of PEP. Bill Edmondson, then with Glaxo agreed to provide the funds for a dinner. The early preceptors, all current preceptors, all school faculty and their spouses were invited. Mrs. Balassone was the guest of honor because Frank was no longer alive. I took this opportunity to speak about Frank and his influence on me as a student, the value of his contributions to pharmacy in Maryland in general, as well as to the establishment of PEP in particular. I was glad I did. Mrs. Balassone sent me a letter expressing her gratitude. Why do we wait until people are dead before we recognize their value?

During my tenure at the school several faculty became more than colleagues. We all know a countless number of people, have numerous acquaintances, and are friendly with many people. Very few people become true friends. True friends are to be treasured. I developed a special relationship with a few of the faculty that I admired and respected. Fred Abramson, Don Fedder, Peter Lamy, Dean Leavitt, Henry Seidman and Ralph Shangraw became real friends. Fred and I were classmates in pharmacy school but our friendship developed after he became a colleague at the school. Fred works extremely hard. His ability to relate to students is special. The school does not give him the credit he deserves but the students certainly do. Don was my mentor when I joined the faculty to direct PEP. He was always available for advice and guidance but he never micromanaged. Don contributes a great deal to the school yet gets little recognition for it. Pete played a significant role in my joining the faculty. He could be intimidating, even when asking the simplest question. I think he enjoyed the reputation. His confidence in me allowed me to experience areas I would not have otherwise. Dean was the chair of the Admissions Committee when I served on it. Choosing those to admit was daunting. The number of well-qualified applicants greatly surpassed the number we could accept. Flipping a coin would provide us with an excellent class. Dean impressed me with his constant endeavor to keep the process as fair as possible. He really cared. Henry cared a great deal about students and the pharmacy profession. He ran the pharmacy practice laboratory and handled the school's continuing education (CE) programs. Henry never got the credit he should have for his efforts putting on continuing education programs. When others attempted it after he died the school ceased developing CE programs. Ralph was the department chair and largely responsible for bringing me onto the faculty and into PEP. He had the ability to manage with authority yet be friendly. Ralph was a "real human being" in the best sense of the words. Pete and Ralph provided PEP with some "clout" with the dean and faculty that I never could. Don, Pete and Ralph were all intimately involved in the Professional Experience Program and a tremendous help from the day I began. Along with Fred, they were among the few on the faculty who always demonstrated an interest in and concern for pharmacy practice and practitioners. I will remember my association with all six of these people forever.

Sometimes you just have to do what you have to do. Two issues arose during the development of the two new doctor of pharmacy programs. The first was just an administrative change. The director would become a coordinator. He would retain responsibilities but lack authority. I knew I would find it difficult to work within such a structure. The second concerned the process of garnering support of the new programs. Changes were made, but not publicized. Although it is not necessary that an employee and employer always agree, every employee has a duty to support his employer publically. I heard objections to these changes from those outside of the school. I could not refute their objections. Therefore, I could not support the school. Therefore, I had no choice.

Compromise regarding a process is acceptable, however nothing justifies compromising a principle. The administrative change involved a process so I did have a choice. However, the program changes involved a principle. Perhaps some thought that in this case the end did justify the means. I did not agree and therefore could not support the school. As much as I liked working there, my only option was to submit my resignation to George Dukes, the department chairman.

I enjoyed the challenges and the variety at the school provided. For the better part of twenty years, I worked the way I work best. Once I know what is needed, let me alone. I will get it done. Having both authority and responsibility makes even the most problematic issues manageable. Disappointed in, but not bitter toward, the school I disassociated myself from the school. I harbor no animosity toward the school or anyone there. They did what they felt they had to do and I did what I had to do.

You would think that by this age I should know that some jobs are just not right for me. While I was contemplating what I would do following my retirement from the school, the Maryland Pharmacists Association announced their Executive Director resigned and they were seeking a successor. A colleague suggested I apply. Without much thought I did. The candidate field narrowed to two. I interviewed several times. I liked the idea of being the head of a statewide organization. Ego, I guess. I was disappointed at coming in second but the only real damage was to my ego. I have to admit I did get some satisfaction when the individual they hired did not work out. However, a job such at this is too political for me. I would not have been good at it and would not have liked it. Not getting the job was good for both me and for the association. What was I thinking?

I know better than to lend money to a friend. While working at Rutkowski's Pharmacy, I became friendly with a sales representative. His father, an over-the-road truck driver, was making more money than he was. He wanted to borrow money for the down payment on a tractor in order to get into the same business. I knew better than to lend money to someone unless I am willing to lose it. It did not occur to me at the time but it is also never a good idea to go into a business I know nothing about with someone I know little about. However, this did seem like a good idea at the time. We formed a partnership, Flagship Motor Express, purchased a tractor and trailer and were in the steel hauling business. We began hauling steel between Baltimore and Pittsburg. My partner, (I'll call him John) got an advance for expenses before leaving. This was deducted from the total amount Flagship was due. The remainder came to me to pay the operational expenses. "John" began taking more and more as an advance and I got less and less to pay bills. I asked the company we hauled for to send me the entire amount and I would give "John" expense money. Their position was that since "Johnn" and I were partners, he had as much right to the money as I did. Unfortunately, "John" always got there first. It got to the point where I did not have sufficient funds to pay the expenses. After many failed attempts, I finally got in touch with "John" and told him I was going to let the bank repossess the tractor and trailer. I got a telephone call from him saying I could have the rig back. The truck was on a diner parking lot and the cashier had the keys. Now what! There is no way possible I could drive this thing.

I contacted another company, Bob's Transport. Bob agreed to help me out by finding a driver and using my rig whenever he could. Fortunately, one of my customers drove a tractor-trailer and took it to Bob's Transport for me.

No long after that "John" came to my house on a motorcycle. He gave me two shopping bags crammed with trip manifests and expense receipts. I have no idea what he expected me to do with them. However, they did make interesting reading. All the manifests were for trips between Baltimore and Pittsburg. However, there were toll receipts from the New Jersey, Massachusetts and Ohio Turnpikes. He was driving the truck but I was taken for a ride.

Bob found drivers and used my truck whenever he could. Each Friday I would go to there, collect what was due me and pay my driver. I was not making any money but at least I could pay the bills. One Wednesday I got a call from Bob. He asked about my driver. It seems he left Monday morning destined for Philadelphia with a load of Coca Cola and cases of tuna fish. It was two days later and the coke and tuna had not arrived. I asked the police to arrest him. They were unable to do anything because no one actually witnessed him drive off. My only alternative was to report the truck stolen. A month went by with no sign of truck or driver. The insurance company paid off the loan. Shortly thereafter, the tractor and empty trailer turned up parked on a street in Philadelphia. There was no sign of the driver. I guess he was home having a tuna sandwich and soda. The good news was the truck now belonged to the insurance company. I was out of the trucking business and glad of it. Yes, I know that I am too trusting. I am not likely to change.

MULTI-LEVEL MARKETING
(I SHOULD KNOW BETTER)

I learned of an Avon type plan for selling home cleaning products door to door. Here was a chance to have other people do all the work and I would make some extra money. I say that now and it seems to good to be true. It was, but it sounded so simple that, "It seemed like a good idea at the time." How could I have been so naïve? There is no way in hell this would work for me. I stopped before I started. The products were actually quite good and Lois had household products that lasted many months.

RETIRED, WELL ALMOST

When I decided to retire from the School of Pharmacy, I knew I wanted to continue to work part time. When offered a full-time position managing a hospital outpatient pharmacy I took it. I liked many things about this job. The outpatient pharmacy was contiguous to the inpatient pharmacy so I had the ability to consult immediately with the clinical pharmacists and had access to their drug information databases. New to me was compounding sterile ophthalmic solutions and injections. I worked with the new medical residents regarding the proper way to write prescriptions. Clinic physicians were concerned about the cost of prescriptions to their patients. We worked together and I determined the most economical of the drugs they were considering. Most satisfying to me was representing pharmacy in a multi-professional pilot program. The object of the program was to determine if it was feasible for to provide for all the services that patients needed either in their homes or at the hospital. The goal was to keep patients at home and out of institutions. We met weekly to review patients' needs and determine the best way to meet them. We provided their medications, medical and dental care, as well as physical and occupational therapy. A van service provided transportation to and from the hospital for day care, medical care, meals and bathing. The program also provided home modifications such as wheel chair ramps when needed.

The outpatient pharmacy dispensed prescription at the request of a caregiver. This was a very inefficient way to provide maintenance medications to a large group of people. My contribution to this aspect was to adapt an institutional pharmacy computer program to facilitate drug distribution to these patients. This made an assembly line approach feasible. The pharmacy automatically provided maintenance medications at four-week intervals. The increased efficiency eased the workload for both the pharmacy and the caregivers.

The downside of this job was that I retired from one full time position to another full time position. Full time jobs always become more than full time. I was starting early and staying late. I began to wonder whether this was a wise choice. The Director of Pharmacy made up my mind for me. He had an abrasive management style. I never experienced it personally, but he never hesitated to chastise an employee in a voice loud enough that everyone in the pharmacy heard. In the midst of what I thought was a discussion regarding something we disagreed on he yelled, "Go into my office and sit" in a tone one might use for a naughty child. As close as I can remember my response was, "I don't think so. I quit. Let one of the inpatient pharmacists finish my shift." Walking out like this was inappropriate and I would change that if I could. On the other hand, the pharmacists and technicians loved me for it because no one ever stood up to him. I went home. Lois came home and knew something was wrong when she saw me mowing the lawn at top speed in the middle of the afternoon. The pharmacists and I always had a good relationship. This episode enhanced it. I was going to the urology clinic at the hospital at the time and always made it a point to visit the pharmacy staff. After I left, they took the user manual I wrote for the computer program I developed and labeled it "MARVIN'S MANUAL" in very large letters. Then they displayed it prominently where the director was certain to see it.

I was not ready to stay home every day but I was ready for a little less work. I approached a chain providing services in community pharmacies, hospitals and institutions and began working on-call at several of their community pharmacies. Community practice had changed from what I remembered. There was more aggravation, particularly because of insurance issues. Although I liked the variety of working in multiple stores, I did not like not knowing when, where or if I was going to work until the last minute.

At a meeting, I met Pat Birmingham, the director of one of the chain's institutional pharmacies providing hospital and nursing home services to a hospital in downtown Baltimore. He offered me a part-time job there and I accepted. There was a regular schedule, I worked with the same staff every day and there was no aggravation from insurance companies or patients. The pharmacy made enteral feedings and was responsible for monitoring/dosing patients taking Coumadin. This gave me the opportunity to do some things I had never done before. I really liked this job.

Driving downtown and parking were the downside. I could not do anything about the drive but I could make a game of parking. Rather than use the parking lot next door I tried to find one of the few places to park on the street. I did it for the challenge not to save money. The pay lot next door was the last resort. I only got two parking tickets. The first was on a very narrow street. I failed to notice the "No Parking" sign posted on the side of the building. That there were no other cars parked nearby should have alerted me. The other ticket was an error. I received a citation for parking in a "No parking after 4:00 PM" zone. The time written on the ticket was 1:15 PM. Even though the officer noted the times on the ticket I expected a bureaucratic nightmare. It was almost disappointing when all it took was one phone call and mailing the ticket back.

One morning I parked next to a Seven-Eleven store, about as far from Deaton as I ever parked. That evening my car would not start. I called AAA for battery service. AAA never arrived by the scheduled time. I called back several times. Still no one arrived. The neighborhood was OK in the daytime but changed dramatically after dark. It began to get dark and the people on the street began looking scruffy. Two men approached, one with a yellow, six-foot snake draped around his neck. I thought I might be the first person ever mugged by a serpent. I was not, they just walked right by but that was enough for me. I called Lois from the Seven-Eleven to pick me up. The next morning I went back for my car and got it started. This position lasted about a year until the hospital closed their nursing home. I was no longer needed.

From there I moved to a pharmacy providing services to a retirement home, nursing home, and hospice. The manager, Wynette Sherard was good to work for. The clinical pharmacist, Jim Salmons and I had frequent interesting discussions. The staff was very nice and very easy to work with. While my mother was there to recuperate following surgery, they stopped and visited with her on my days off. This job lasted until the institution awarded the contract to another provider.

I had the option of going from there back to community pharmacy or to their institutional pharmacy serving nursing homes throughout the state. I knew I did not want to go back into community practice so I chose to go to the institutional pharmacy in spite of its reputation as being very hectic. This is a big operation. On the day shift most of my responsibility involved checking the technicians' work. Checking is important but mind numbing work. In addition, there is constant push to get work out quickly in order to meet the frequent delivery schedules. Working at a fast pace increases the potential to miss a technician's error, thus making it my error. The evening shift was less hectic, the staff more congenial and the variety of tasks greater. Working evenings was more interesting and therefore a pleasure. However, I was not going to do it on a regular basis. I was not going to work evenings, did not enjoy days and did not want to go back to community pharmacy; it was time to think about moving on.

For a time, I had a pharmacist's part-time "dream job." While thinking about what I should do when I moved on, I received a telephone call from a manager I had previously worked for. The pharmacy she was now managing needed a part-time pharmacist. The pharmacy had a grant to dispense prescription drugs, provided free by manufacturers to needy patients who were without insurance and not eligible for Medicaid. Social workers qualified the patient based on each manufacturer's criteria and obtained the necessary prescriptions from the physician. Delivery direct from the manufacturer to the patient took several weeks. The pharmacy filled and delivered the prescriptions immediately. At the end of each month, the manufacturers replaced the drugs we dispensed. This was a nine to five, five-day a week, closed holidays operation and my schedule was flexible. There were no patients, physicians or insurance companies to deal with. This was the ideal job for a pharmacist who wanted no aggravation. In addition, I was helping the needy. A grant decrease resulted in a reduction of staff. I was the last hired and therefore the first to go. I was disappointed when this happened because I really enjoyed working there. No one likes to fire people; it is sometimes necessary. It may be the most distasteful task in management but is sometimes. Med-Bank continued to reduce pharmacy staff and the last I heard was that there was intent to close the pharmacy aspect of the operation.

    I was still not ready to retire completely. I met an ex-student who was now a pharmacy supervisor for a chain store. She offered me a part time position. I was skeptical of going back to community practice. However, I accepted this position because the store was nearby, not overly busy, open shorter hours than most, and had competent technicians and pharmacists who would be flexible regarding my schedule. Both the technicians and pharmacists had been there a long time and their relationship with patients was more like those of the neighborhood pharmacies early in my career. If there was a community pharmacy that was a viable option, this should be it. At least it was worth a try. It was a perfect fit at the time. However, the chair began losing market share and felt it necessary to become more competitive. Typical of corporate responses, the first step was to lower costs by reducing salary expenses. As a result, fewer people began doing more work. I was concerned that the pressure to fill prescriptions so quickly was increasing the risk of errors. The next step was to close some of the smaller stores. This store was among the first to go. I could have stayed with the chain but any store I went to would be busier, open longer hours and have similar staffing issues. The stress and frustration of working under these conditions was no longer acceptable. I was out of realistic options. It was time to retire completely.

The most difficult thing about being an employee after being in charge for so many years is the lack of control. You've undoubtedly heard the saying, "There's a right way, a wrong way and the army way." Owners believe, "There is a right way, the wrong way and my way. We'll do it my way."

TRAVEL—AN ADVENTURE WAITING TO HAPPEN

Travel is one of my two favored leisure activities. (The other is playing in a band.) I always liked being anywhere that I have never been before. Growing up I liked the trips I took with my parents or grandparents. After we married, Lois and I have had the good fortune to visit many places.

My only train trip as a youngster was to Atlantic City with my mother and her cousin Naomi Zipp. This was during World War II. The train passed the Glenn L. Martin Company and I knew my father was at work there. Trains were crowded at the time because gas rationing limited automobile travel. There were no empty seats. Men were sitting on suitcases or standing in the aisle.

I am sure we went on the beach but the only activity I remember in Atlantic City is playing miniature golf and riding a bicycle on the boardwalk. I watched fighter pilots practice shooting at a targets towed by another plane. The military built towers on the beach to direct artillery fire at German submarines. The towers, never used, remained for many years.

After the war ended in 1945 there were a few automobile trips with my parents before my decision that I rather stay home than travel with them. One summer we drove to Niagara Falls and crossed the bridge into Canada. Coming back, I thought it was neat to see a sign saying, "To the United States." On a trip to Luray Caverns and the Skyline Drive, we stayed at a motel in Harrisonburg, Virginia. We took what we needed for the night and left the remainder in the car. During the night, someone broke a window and stole all our clothing from the car. My father drove back home. We got more clothes and resumed the trip.

I liked camping from my very first experience in boy scouts. The year after Lois and I married, I went camping with George Mill (we met on our honeymoon) and two of his friends. It was late summer but still warm. We took bathing suits, expecting to swim. We arrived and learned the camp was closing for the season. We decided to stay anyway and set up our tent. The next day the park rangers shut off the water, locked the bathhouses, the bathrooms and their offices and left. We were the only ones in the park. We had no facilities, but we had an entire state park to ourselves. The lake we camped by was our only source of water. This was near Lake Placid, New York, not far from the Canadian border. The first night the temperature went from balmy to freezing. Unprepared but undaunted we wore several layers of clothing, both day and night. We hiked and canoed during the day. At night, we slept in our clothes and tried to get a little heat into the tent by building a fire in front. We got more smoke than heat. It was too cold to bathe. To say we were "unkempt" by mid-week would be an understatement. We drove to a Howard Johnson's Restaurant in Lake Placid. I cannot imagine what they thought when we walked in. The four of us went into their men's room to wash and shave. We looked like vagrants. I am surprised they didn't call the police. We left without even buying anything. I feel certain there was a sigh of relief when we did. We spent the rest of the week in the park. It is safe to say that Lois is glad she missed one of my most memorable camping experiences.

Some of our earliest vacations after we married involved camping. All included Lois, Gregory and Leslie. Lois is not the outdoor type by any stretch of the imagination. Nevertheless, I have to say she was an extremely good sport about camping. We usually rented a tent top trailer, so there was no need to sleep on the ground.

I did the cooking and cleaning up because this is part of the fun of camping. Most parks have campsites set up around a central bathhouse and bathroom facilities. Each morning every camper starts the day using these facilities, usually bleary eyed and unkempt in a ratty bathrobe. That is, all but one. Lois never left our tent until perfectly groomed, with her make-up perfect, hair in place and neatly dressed in shorts or slacks.

It seems that every camping trip included at least one adventure. The four of us were on our way to Deep Creek Lake when the trailer hitch snapped. Fortunately, the trailer ran off the road to the right and not into traffic. I went back to a business we passed a mile or two earlier to ask where I could find someone who could weld the hitch together. By luck, a welder happened to be working in the basement. He left this job and went back to the trailer with me. After he removed the hitch, he took the pieces to his home where he straightened them and welded them together. Then he came back and reattached the hitch. How much was all this going to cost? I just hoped I had enough money. His response when I asked was, "Is five dollars to much?" That was incredible, even for the early 1960's.

Equally incredible was when I returned the trailer they refused to give me the five dollars because I did not have a receipt. I told them I did not have the nerve to ask for a receipt after all the work he did for five dollars. The repair was obvious, but that did not matter. Livid, I went back to my car and wrote a receipt myself. They gave me five dollars. Unbelievable.

Rain is one thing that really puts a damper (no pun intended) on camping. We drove to Swallow Falls on a bright sunny day and set up our tent. The next morning it was raining when we woke up. It was still raining when we went to bed. It rained every day after except the day we left. We drove home in bright sunshine.

The mosquitoes on Maryland's Eastern Shore seem much worse than in Baltimore. Shad Landing State Park is located near Berlin, Maryland. The mosquitoes there were the worst I ever encountered.

They didn't bother us during the day, so we had a good time. At night, they were ferocious. They ignored the repellent and bit through heavy clothing. Lois wore heavy slacks and hose the entire time but the mosquitoes got to her anyway. Gregory, Leslie and I had many bites. Lois had the most. She counted nearly a hundred welts on her legs.

We spent a week camping in Cedarville State Forest is near Brandywine, Maryland. Across Route 301 from Cedarville State Forest is a riding stable. Going for a horseback ride through the woods sounded like fun. As we walked from the parking lot a horse came racing toward us with the rider yelling, "Look out, get out of the way." You would think that would have dissuaded us, but it did not. Gregory, Leslie, Lois and I mounted up and started out. My horse veered off the path. I tried to turn him back and he reared up. They told me, "Be careful, that horse has a sore mouth." About the same time, the cinch on Gregory's horse came loose and the saddle slid off. That was enough for me. Lois and Leslie went on while Gregory and I waited at the barn. An hour later, we watched as Lois and Leslie slowly ambled back toward the barn. Everything had gone well for them. Then a horse and rider leaving the barn accidently brushed Leslie's horse as he went by. Startled, Leslie's horse took off at top speed heading toward Route 301. Leslie was holding on for dear life. It did not help when one stable boy said, "I feel sorry for that girl" and another said, "It would be better if she fell off." I had visions of them running in front of a speeding truck on Highway 301. What else could I do but run after her. A running man is never going to catch a running horse under any circumstances and here I was trying to run through honeysuckle brush about two feet deep. Leslie managed to hold on until another rider caught up with them and brought them back. She was unhurt, but her muscles ached for days.

Neither Lois nor I had been on a cruise before we were married. A few years after we were married, I saw a Towson Travel Agency advertisement for cruises. The two cruises to Bermuda appealed to us. Both left the same day, one from New York and the other from

Washington, DC. There was little difference in the cost. Towson travel told me the boats were similar, but the one leaving from New York was a 'little larger.' We chose the Washington cruise because it was much more convenient. Gregory and Leslie stayed with Harry and Edna. Our scheduled departure time was 5:00 PM. We left in the morning to get to arrive early at the dock. It was a good thing we did. I opened the trunk of the car and found one bag was missing. It was my fault; I left our hang-up bag at home. Every dressy outfit for Lois was still on Hilltop Ave. I suggested we just buy something in Bermuda. Lois was hysterical, what was she going to wear to the affairs on the boat. Fortunately, it was Saturday and Harry was home. We called and he picked up the bag and brought it to the ship. There was not much time to spare but we made it and Lois had her dressy outfits.

Our cabin was small; I could touch both walls with my fingertips. It had bunk beds because a full size bed would not fit. If that was not bad enough, there was no private bath. It never occurred to me to ask about that. The boat was already on its way down the Potomac so there was no turning back; we might as well make the best of it. As we walked on deck, the steward was assigning deck chairs. We were in our mid-twenties and there were old women in the first dozen or so chairs. I asked for chairs further aft, hoping the younger people would be there. Following dinner, at a table with a grumpy woman and her gracious but quiet husband, we went back on deck to meet some of our shipmates. There was an occupant in every deck chair. Everyone appeared to be at least seventy years old except for a few teenagers. We learned there were two groups aboard. One was a group of retired schoolteachers and the other a female Sea Scout troop.

They served tea and cookies daily on deck but they could never seem to get the tea, cookies, cream, lemon and sugar out all at the same time. It was either eat dry cookies or drink cold tea. Every dinner was mediocre. Think White Coffee Pot. We were not on the Love Boat.

The only place to buy anything was a shop about the size of a closet.

It was only open a few hours each afternoon. They sold odds and ends such as toothpaste and seasick pills. Candy bars were the only food for sale.

We did manage to meet four other "young" couples on the boat. They were about twenty years older but at least we could commiserate with each other. At night we got together in the only bar and had a few drinks. When I asked for some peanuts or snacks the waitress brought a handful of peanuts in what appeared to be an ashtray, put them on the table and said, "Don't tell anyone where you got these." We attempted to dance. The weather was not bad but the Evangeline was so small that the floor moved so much it was impossible to keep time with the music. The ten of us became friends because there was no one else even close to our ages.

They tried to fill the swimming pool several times on the way to Bermuda. It was not rough but once there was two feet of water in the pool, it began to splash out. The only time water stayed in the pool was when we were in port. We met our friends about ten o'clock one morning and decided we had just witnessed the highlight of the day; watching the garbage as it was thrown overboard. What else could we do? Not much. There was a costume party one night. Lois and I dressed as Romans in togas and won first prize.

We hoped things would get better once we got to Bermuda. We docked in St. George. While we waited to disembark, Lois encountered a sobbing young woman. Her father died earlier that morning. We had to wait until authorities cleared the ship before anyone could go ashore. Lois consoled the woman while the ship's officers complained about the paper work. We finally disembarked, and took a taxi to Hamilton. There is nothing in St. George; to do anything required a taxi ride. On our first trip to Hamilton, we saw the ship from New York that we could have been on. It docked right on the main street in Hamilton, just steps away from everything. The travel agent said it was a little bigger. This was about ten times the size of the Evangeline. If the Evangeline held three hundred passengers, this must have held thirteen hundred. I am sure they had more than one bar, plenty of peanuts, actual shops, real activities and real entertainment. The price for the convenience was high.

The last day in Bermuda, all five couples spent the day together on one of the nicest beaches ever. The sand was clean and the water was clear and warm. Then it was back to the ship for our evening departure. The first night out was the captain's dinner. On every table was a bottle of champagne. The weather was not rough but people came in, sat down and then left a few minutes later. I guess they lost their sea legs while in port. Their seasickness was our gain. As people left, we gathered up their champagne. One couple had a larger cabin than the rest. Everyone had a larger cabin than we did. We took all the champagne to their cabin and had a party. What we were unable to drink we packed in our suitcases to bring home.

What a trip. The cruise ship was a disaster waiting to happen. It was tiny; there are larger boats in the inner harbor. The engineer took a liking to us and showed us the engine room. He was very proud of his job and told us, "This is where the real captain is." We learned from him that the cabins were so small because where once there was one cabin now there were two. The ship, designed to hold 150 passengers now held 300. On the other hand, Bermuda was very nice. We made friends on the cruise that we later visited while traveling.

We docked in Washington and disembarked into a giant warehouse. Luggage, sorted alphabetically, lined the warehouse. It took a while to find ours because it was in several different places. Oed is only three letters but it seems to cause a lot of difficulty. As we struggled with our luggage someone asked, "Are you Mr. Oed?" It seems that in the process of taking our car to a car wash (included with the valet parking) an accident damaged the radiator. A sealant temporarily stopped the leak. They said I should have the radiator fixed properly and send the bill to them. We passed Belair Road Chevrolet on the way home. I decided to stop and schedule the repair. The first thing I noticed was water running out of the radiator. We were lucky to make it all the way from Washington before this happened. I left the car there for repairs. Harry was there when we needed him the day we left and there again the day we got back. He picked us up and drove us home.

A year or so later we learned the Evangeline burned and sank. We have been on a number or very nice cruises but none with as many stories to tell as the Evangeline.

Initially at Rutkowski's Pharmacy, I utilized graduate students from the UMAB School of Pharmacy as relief pharmacists. One summer I arranged coverage between two graduate students and took off an entire month. We bought a station wagon and borrowed a mattress that fit in the back. Off we went to visit friends in Santa Maria, California. We took an ice chest, bought food along the way and had picnic lunches. This gave Gregory and Leslie, about four and five years old at the time, an opportunity to run off some energy. They played on the mattress during the day and slept on it while we drove at night. Sometimes we drove all night while they slept. This was a fun way to travel. This was before seat belts and before there was an awareness of the safety issues of riding unrestrained. Along the way, we visited the Grand Canyon, Meteor Crater, every cowboy or Indian attraction, and anything of interest that we passed. We stayed with our friends, Sharon and Ed, in Santa Maria. One day we went to a Pacific Ocean beach. The water was so cold no one went in above his ankles. Before leaving for San Francisco, we spent two days at Disneyland with the Ed, Sharon and their kids. We drove to San Francisco to visit Tedd, who would later marry Lois's sister. However, we were unable to contact him at his apartment and continued on our way. When we got home, we learned that at the time we were there he was in the hospital having an emergency appendectomy.

On our way from San Francisco to visit Sequoia National Forest, we made a spur of the moment decision to try camping. We already had an ice chest. We bought a blanket, a pot, several beach towels and food and were off for Sequoia, Yellowstone and Mt. Rushmore. Our station wagon substituted as our tent. The mattress in the back was our bed and the towels covered the windows for privacy.

Some of the redwood trees have been growing in Sequoia for more than two thousand years. They are huge. Many of their trunks are much wider than a car. A tunnel, cut through one tree, is a tourist attraction. We were able to drive our car through the tree. Many are as tall as 350 feet. Lois and I kept pointing out just how tall the trees were. Leslie was more interested in pointing out little ones just starting to grow.

In Sequoia, bears roamed around the car at night sniffing and snorting. In the campsite opposite ours, a bear rooted through the containers stored on a car roof while the campers watched from their tent. They were lucky; he could have been inside their tent looking for food. At least our station wagon was bear proof. During the night, Lois heard a noise and saw a bear looking at her through the car window. What does one do if there is a need to use the bathroom during the night? The next day, while Lois and I were walking in Sequoia with Gregory and Leslie, we wondered what to do should we encounter a bear. We never did so it never became an issue.

Our next stop was Yellowstone Park where the bears are losing their fear of people. Signs warn everyone not to feed bears and to keep car windows closed. It seemed that more people ignored the warnings than obeyed them. We kept our car windows closed because bears would come right up to stopped cars looking for a handout. Some people did feed them. One man got out of his car to take a close-up picture of a mother bear with two cubs. Nothing happened but that could have ended tragically. We were feeling superior because we were obeying the restrictions. I heard a noise from the back seat. A bear reached through the open rear window (I forgot to close that one) and his claws hooked in a seat cushion. Leslie and the bear were having a tug of war. Lois yelled to Leslie to let go of the cushion. As I put the car in gear, the bear's claws came free and he jumped down. That was a narrow escape. Leslie could have been hurt.

The most scenic camping area is just below Yellowstone Falls. We were disappointed to find it full. We were told about an area further up the mountain that had space but, "did not have all of the amenities" of the main campground. We arrived and found space, but not much else. We were alone and there was nothing I would call an 'amenity.' We were there two days and did not encounter another person. There was a fireplace, a table, a Port-a-Pot and a stream. Our water came from the stream. In the main camping area, people were walking around in shorts or in bathing suits and swimming. The higher we went up the mountain the cooler it got. There was snow on the ground where we camped. I have movies of Leslie in a sun suit making snowballs. The following morning while eating breakfast a small herd of deer walked across the stream and right past us. The view of Yellowstone Falls is spectacular but I am glad there was no camping space and we had to come here. We were in our own world.

A cruise is like a party with the captain as the designated driver. There is much to do, yet it is so relaxing. You go to bed at night; in the morning, you are somewhere else. The best part is that your room, restaurant and entertainment travel with you. If our first cruise was a fiasco, our second was the opposite. Baltimore Lutheran School, where Douglas attended, had fund raising auctions. The Caribbean cruise I bought there was my first experience with a travel agency obtaining airline tickets. Lois and I arrived at the airport early and waited at the gate to board. As we were about to about to board, the agent stopped us and said we had to check in at the counter. This could not be good. It never occurred to me that check-in was necessary because the tickets had seat numbers on them. The counter agent said he reassigned our seats because we had not checked in on time. Panic set in. We had to get to Ft. Lauderdale; our ship was sailing that afternoon. There was a pause while a hundred things flashed through my mind. Then he said, "I guess the only thing I can do is put you in first class." I wavered between thanking him for getting us on the airplane and giving us first class seats or berating him for not telling me that in the first place.

This is the only time I remember flight attendants being funny. They seemed to have an amusing way to relate the instructions about seat belts, oxygen masks, using the bathroom and water landings. I thought everything they said was hysterically funny; no one else seemed to. Maybe it was just my relief that we made it on that airplane at all.

This was our first trip on a real cruise ship. We thoroughly enjoyed the Caribbean and were impressed with Holland-America Lines' service.

Because we enjoyed our first Caribbean cruise with Holland-America so much, when they offered another leaving from Baltimore, we decided to see another part of the Caribbean. Leaving from Baltimore was great because it was so convenient. There were no long trips to get to the dock and back and no airline flights. The last day of the cruise Lois won a free cruise playing bingo. The following year we went to the Caribbean again. It was a nice trip but perhaps one too many to the same area.

One summer the Maryland Pharmacists Association sponsored a cruise through the Panama Canal. The canal operation is astounding. I stood on the bow of our ship and watched the cruise ship in the lock in front of us rise up higher than my head. Train engines tow ships through the locks, some with only inches to spare.

It took less than an hour to complete a pharmacy continuing education program on the ship. There was no real "program." This just qualified part of the cost as a business expense. We just answered the quiz questions as a group. This was not education and inappropriate for a professional organization.

We spent a few hours shopping in Cartegena, Columbia. Street vendors hawked gold and silver chains, watches and jewelry. They were more persistent than any I had ever seen; following us down the street, gradually lowering the price and insisting whatever they were selling was an enormous bargain. I dislike this immensely. I doubted the wisdom of going to Cartegena because of the history of drug trafficing and violence in Columbia. Nothing happened but the open trucks loaded with armed soldiers riding by periodically did nothing to alleviate my anxiety.

While having dinner with them, Ron and Joan Resch showed us a brochure for a Boumi Shriners (this was before I belonged) cruise to Scandinavian capitals. Lois could not understand why they did not intend to go. Two days later Joan called. Lois was so enthusiastic about the trip they reconsidered. Now they were going and asked if we wanted to go along. We said yes immediately.

Our first stop was London. We stayed there London for several days and did some sightseeing before taking a bus to the cruise ship. We rode on the London EYE, the largest ferris wheel (443 feet tall) in Europe.

The tour began in London. We took a side trip to Greenwich. At a stripe marking the International Date Line we stood with one foot in Sunday and the other in Monday.

From London, we went to Birmingham to board our ship. As we set sail, we could see the cliffs of Dover. As in the World War II song, they really are white. Things like this fascinate me.

We sailed to Germany, Estonia, Finland, Estonia, Russia, Finland and Sweden. Ours was the first cruise of the year going though the Kiel Canal in Germany. Some people sat on the banks in lawn chairs and waved as we passed others rode bicycles on a path beside the canal. Was this their entertainment? They are either laid back or the need to get a life. The smoke stacks on the ship tilted so the ship could pass beneath the low bridges over the canal. The first morning I met Joan having breakfast in the dining room. Joan's husband Ron likes to sleep in and so does my wife Lois. We met this way several times. We enjoyed the entire trip. Lois and I entered a golf tournament in one of the lounges. Lois, who never played golf in her life, not only beat me, she won the tournament. The Hermitage and the palaces in St. Petersburg were the most incredible part of this experience.

We took two other trips with Ron and Joan. One was a cruise to

Nova Scotia and the other a bus trip through the northeast. Although there are some similarities, I prefer cruises to bus trips. Cruises are much more relaxing. There is little to do on a bus other than look out the window. Cruise ships do much of their traveling at night and when they are at sea, there are always activities.

I was fortunate that the positions I held often facilitated travel. Medicine Shoppe International (MSI) was a family oriented organization. Their annual meetings always provided something for spouses and children and took place in cities that offered something of interest to tourists.

Several of our vacations were extensions of Medicine Shoppe meetings. Harry and Edna kept Douglas; he was still a baby, while Gregory and Leslie attended MSI's Atlanta meeting with us. We stayed at a new, and very classy, Hyatt Regency Hotel. There was a huge lobby with an atrium. The elevators were all glass and on the outside of the building. The design was a new concept at the time and visitors frequently came just to look at the elevators, lobby and atrium. We arrived early in the morning and visited Atlanta Underground before it was open. It was eerie. The lighting was dim and almost no one else was there. The echoes of our footsteps made it sound like an old Jack the Ripper movie. At that time, Atlanta Underground was an active tourist center and very safe. Gregory and Leslie, about 14 and 15, were old enough that we dropped them off there in the afternoon and let them come back to the hotel by taxi.

Lois asked the hotel restaurant to fix a plate without meat for Leslie. What she got was a plate with an assortment of vegetables so imaginatively arranged that it appeared to be a work of art. The chef outdid himself and even came to our table. The chef asked, "Is the little girl all right?" It seems he thought Leslie could not eat meat because she was ill. We never told him otherwise.

One of the more memorable was the meeting in Saint Louis, the corporate headquarters for MSI. They went all out. In one large room was an arcade set up for the kids. The machines did not require money to operate. It was a good experience for Douglas who was about nine at the time. Kids who never met before got along without a problem. They willingly shared time at the popular games, etc. We had lunch on a paddle wheel riverboat, saw the Clydesdale horses, and went to the museum below and took the elevator to the top of the Gateway Arch. MSI hired two paddle wheel boats for a dinner cruise. A race developed between them on the way back. On casino night, we all received play money for the games of chance. Later that night there was a "play money" auction. The first item auctioned was a refrigerator. No one believed the auction was for real and the refrigerator went cheap, especially since this was play money. Only after it was over did anyone realize the auction was real. Someone was going home with a refrigerator. The highlight was the auction of a TV. Now everyone knew this was real. The bids got beyond the amount any one individual had. Individuals began pooling their money. Then tables pooled their money. Finally, entire regions pooled their money. The Maryland region won and gave the TV to our regional manager who had just gotten married.

The big hit however, was the speaker, introduced as the Educational Advisor to the Queen of England. He was in the USA for an international conference and agreed to speak at our meeting. He was the most attention-grabbing speaker I ever heard and had many interesting things to say. Then he began telling amusing things that happened to him as a first time visitor to the United States. The events became funnier and funnier. It finally occurred to me that this could not all happen to one person on one trip. Near the end, he lost his British accent, admitted he was not British and in a drawl said, "My name is Saxet and I am from Texas." (Texas spelled backwards is Saxet.) Then, losing the southern drawl he said his real name and where he really was from. At least, I think this last one was real. How would I know?

Earlier that morning there was a breakfast and fashion show for the women. As I began to tell Lois about our speaker, she interrupted to tell me she knew all about him. The women had breakfast with an advisor to the Queen of England and that she knew he was going to speak to us. He had been at the breakfast, British accent and all. He left them to come to our meeting with no one the wiser.

One summer Miami Beach was the location for a national MSI meeting. Some of the meetings were right on the beach. As always, MSI allowed time to do touristy things. In addition to enjoying the beach, we saw the dolphins at the Seaquarium and other attractions.

Ocean City, Maryland has an excellent beach. Although Lois and I are not "beach people," we went several times when Gregory and Leslie were teenagers and Douglas was very young. Gregory and Leslie would each take a friend. The four teenagers went to the beach and boardwalk and were on their own most of the time. Each evening they would watch Douglas while Lois and I went to a restaurant for dinner.

A second floor apartment where we stayed had a fire escape on the outside. I saw a figure on the fire escape go past a window. It was one of Gregory's friends. He came in through the window to get out of the rain. I sent him out. The last I saw of him he was sitting on the curb in the rain. Lois insists I let him stay and sleep on the sofa but I don't remember it that way.

Another time when we returned from dinner there were four people outside the motel. We recognized Leslie and the two friends who came with us but not the other girl. Where was Gregory? He was the other girl. While we were away, Leslie and her friend made him up to look like a girl. No one would have known he was a male.

Another year, Douglas didn't want to go back to the motel when it was time for us to return from dinner. He agreed to go when Gregory told him there was a horse there. The others walked back with Douglas while Gregory ran ahead. When the others got to the motel, there was Gregory down on his hands and knees with a sheet over him, pretending to be a horse. Douglas was terrified and just screamed.

The Maryland Pharmacists Association (MPhA) sponsored a tour to Paris. Except for Canada and the Caribbean, this was our first trip out of the country. Lee (Lois' cousin) and her husband Bob went with us. Our flight landed in Brussels due to bad weather in Paris. An announcement said a bus would take us to Paris, but gave no directions to find this bus. I recognized someone from our plane as he went through an exit door. Hoping he knew where he was going we followed. Outside was a long line of parked busses. We checked the bus windows as we walked by and chose one of the busses with occupants we recognized. Part way to Paris the bus had mechanical problems and stopped in a service area for repairs. After about two hours, we were back on our way. Then, instead of taking us to our hotel, the driver took us to the Paris airport. The busses that were to take us to the hotel may have been at that airport in the morning, but they were not there now. There were several long discussions between the tour guide, the driver and bus officials in Brussels. The driver finally got permission and took us to our hotel.

By now, it was well after dinnertime. We checked in and went immediately to their restaurant. I remember the meal as being very good, but that could have been because, other than a snack at the service area, we had not eaten since breakfast on the airplane. The bill came. In France, the tip is included in the bill. Sometimes a diner leaves a few additional francs for special service. I forgot and calculated an additional 15% tip. To compound my mistake I told Bob the amount and we both put in an additional 15%. The waiter ended up with 30% of the total check in addition to the tip that was included. The meal cost a lot more than it should have but my mistake came in handy the following morning. Lee needed something to eat before we went to breakfast. I asked the hostess in the restaurant if I could have one or two rolls. She refused. Our waiter from the night before overheard the conversation and got the rolls for me. We never saw him again. It may be just as well. He would have been very disappointed with his next tip.

Maybe it was our first time in Europe, or maybe it was Paris, but

I recall being in awe as we walked along the Left Bank. Lee and I glanced at each other and simultaneously said, "I can't believe I'm really here." Contrary to what we heard, the French were very cordial to us. On one occasion, Bob paid the taxi fare. The driver counted the money, said "Too much," and gave some back. Would it happen that way in Baltimore?

We were friendly with a couple from Washington who had a letter of introduction to the chef at the Jacqes Cagne restaurant. They invited us to have lunch with them there. It was classy. We ordered wine and Lois ordered her usual Coke. The wine steward, with a towel over his arm, brought her coke and presented with great flourish. It was great fun. Suddenly I felt very strange and went downstairs to the men's room. It was in use. As I waited, I fainted. I leaned against the wall and could feel myself beginning to slide. The next thing I remember is someone helping me off the floor. This was a first for me. I sat there a few minutes, began feeling better and went back to our table. Lois said I did not look good. I was no longer sick but afraid to eat anything. By the end of lunch, I was fine. We walked around Paris the rest of the afternoon. I surprised Lois that night when I told her what happened. She was incredulous and said, "Do you mean you fell down?"

Another first was a pickpocket taking money from me on a Metro (subway) train. One man standing in the doorway blocked my way as I was about to get off. I felt something touching my back pocket and realized what was happening. I whacked at the hand reaching in my pocket, pushed the other man out of the way and jumped off. I thought I had foiled their effort. Alerted to the frequency of this type of theft, my wallet, passport and most of my money was in a money belt. My French dictionary was in my back pocket where my wallet would normally be. A small amount of cash was in a side pants pocket. I thought he was after the dictionary thinking it was my wallet. Wrong. That was a diversion. All the money (not very much) in my side pocket was gone. How did he know the money was there? How did he get to it without my knowing? After that, I was always wary when in a crowd.

Lee and Bob were always good traveling companions. We always had a good time together. I liked to disagree with Lee because I always knew what to say that would get her started. We especially enjoyed going to theme weekends at the Hershey Hotel. Lee and I looked forward to the sing-along in the hotel lounge. I probably embarrassed Lois. We had become very close. Bob asked me to speak at Lee's funeral. This was a difficult thing to do but felt it an honor that I was asked. Lois and I still think of Lee often.

As a faculty member of the UMAB School of Pharmacy, I attended meetings in cities throughout the United States. This was an opportunity to see the country. Frequently Lois went along. We often extended our stay to make it a vacation. We saw Boston, Salt Lake City, Dallas, San Francisco, New Orleans, San Antonio and Charleston this way. We went to Boston during one of the worst heat spells in history. Rooms were hot because the air conditioners were unable to handle the high temperatures. Some quit altogether. We rode in several taxis with non-functioning air conditioners. Everyone was complaining. One day Lois and Douglas went sightseeing while I went to a meeting. They told me about a park where many people were walking into a pool with their clothes, sometimes even dressy clothes or suits, on to try to cool off. The next day they wanted me to see this spectacle but we could not find any pool. The TV news that night cleared up the mystery. The city closed all the swimming pools because the lifeguards were on strike. They began going to the park instead. The city then drained the pool in the park because there was no fence to keep people out.

Don Fedder was unable to consult for Timex and asked if I was interested. I was. Lois and I took this as an opportunity to visit New York City. I consulted for Timex Corporation regarding two new digital products, a bathroom scale and a blood pressure monitor. This was about 1978. Part of my compensation was a scale and a blood pressure monitor. The best was a Timex watch, with *"Marvin Oed"* in place of the Timex name. That made it unique. I really liked the watch. It was, according to the literature, *"The World's Thinnest Quartz Calendar Watch."* Some years later, I could not find a replacement battery and the watch disappeared. Both Lois and I forgot about it. After all these years, it just reappeared. Lois accidently came upon it just last month (November 2008). I am wearing it again because I really like it.

Travel with friends can make travel special. What began as a collegial relationship with Don Fedder at the school of pharmacy became a very close, personal relationship with Don and his wife Michaeline. During a break for dessert while playing bridge, Don casually asked if we had a vacation planned. Equally casually, I said no but that I always wanted to go to Australia. Don said he always wanted to go there too. That night we decided to together. I like people who make decisions without a lot of unnecessary thought. Since we were traveling so far and unlikely to go a second time, we expanded the trip to include New Zealand. Our travel agent recommended a three day add on in Fiji because we would want time to rest at the end. We added Fiji to our itinerary. When we arrived in Australia our Tauck guide said, "This is not a vacation, it's a tour." How right he was! Don and Michaeline are great travel companions. There was not a cross word the entire month. In fact, I believe we became even closer friends as a result. This was a great experience. However, after seventeen flights and all the bus rides and side trips it was time to unwind. All we wanted to do at the end was relax. Fiji was the perfect spot for that.

Australia is so vast that most of our travel there was by airplane. We visited a cattle ranch so large, (a million acres) that cowboys used helicopters instead of horses. In remote areas the 'flying doctors' make house calls by airplane. New Zealand was the more picturesque country. I thought about bungee jumping while in New Zealand, but then decided that a jet boat was a safer alternative. There was a billboard suggesting that people with a back problem should not go. Lois wisely decided not to go. It was exciting. Sometimes the boat raced at a rock wall and veered off at the last second with just inches to spare. Other times the driver spun the boat around so the bow would dip down and barely make it under an overhanging rock. It was thrilling; I never felt unsafe or I would not be smiling in a picture they took. A day later, we read that one of the boats crashed into the rocks and one person died.

While In New Zealand Tauck arranged for a couple to pick the four of us up and take us to have dinner and spend the evening at their home. This was unexpected but wonderful. Our hosts were delightful; the six of us had a wonderful evening.

We didn't do much in Fiji but we did take a floatplane over the nearby islands. This is the only time I flew with a barefoot pilot.

Tauck did such a great job on our Australia trip that when their brochure describing the Galapagos trip came, there was no thought to using any other travel agent. While getting some vaccinations at a Travel Clinic the advisory papers warned of the dangers of pickpockets, going into parks, taxi drivers who robbed passengers and kidnappings. This made us more than a little anxious. A Tauck agent said none of their previous tours had any problems. The kidnappings involved political issues and drug dealers, not tourists. They offered to refund our deposit or arrange another tour. Rather than cance, we decided to go with the tour grout rather that a day earlier as planned.

We stayed overnight at a Comfort Inn near BWI to avoid rushing for an early morning flight. Chuck Flathman, a friend of Gregory and Leslie, worked in the restaurant there at the time and reserved a room for us. It only cost us $25.00 because Chuck told them I was his uncle. We ate dinner in the restaurant. Lois asked to have her Pepsi replaced three times because it tasted funny. Finally, it occurred to me the Diamox we took to prevent altitude sickness was the likely cause. I told the waiter that the last Pepsi tasted much better.

I am glad that we made the change in arrival plans. We landed in

Quito late at night. Customs, Immigration and baggage claim are all in one large room. The baggage from our flight was stacked in the middle of the floor. Signs were in Spanish and the process was not clear. No one seemed to speak English. I was not certain where to go or what to do. Cab drivers were in the area aggressively trying to hustle fares. A man pointed to the pile of luggage and said "American?" Assuming he meant the American Airline flight we arrived on; I pointed out our bags. He carried them to the customs/immigration line. A few seconds later, another man tapped me on the shoulder and motioned for me to follow him. He picked up our bags and carried them out the door. I expected someone to stop us but nobody did. No one checked passports or anything. Taxi drivers pounced on each traveler as he exited. I was very glad to see our Tauck guide there to meet us. She guided us through all the commotion to their van and took us to the hotel were we checked in and met the others in our tour group.

We crossed the equator several times in Ecuador. At one monument, we stood over a yellow line marking the equator. We stood with one foot in the northern and the other foot in the southern hemisphere.

Ecuador is a beautiful, mountainous country. Because of its location on the equator, there are no seasonal changes in Ecuador. Sunrise and sunset occur at the same time all year. Virtually everything can be grown there. The altitude determines where specific things can be grown.

The city of Quito is in a valley but is still over 9,000 feet above sea level. We went to lunch on the rim of a dormant volcano at 18,000 feet. Taking the Diamox helped, but we still got breathless climbing a long flight of steps to the restaurant.

The last morning we were there, the presidents of Columbia and Ecuador met in our hotel. In addition to the regular security, there were intimidating looking men in dark suits, sunglasses, earphones and curious bulges in their jackets.

I had two years of Spanish in high school but remember very little other than, "Un burro es un animal." It wasn't very likely that this would come up in a conversation. Before leaving home, I learned some common Spanish words and phrases. When it came time to check out I practiced what I would say.

At the counter the conversation was something like:

MLO:	Quiero pagar la cuenta por favor.
CLERK:	Yes. What is your room number?
MLO:	Cinco dos uno.
CLERK:	Any other charges?
MLO:	Cen en Café Quito.

Suddenly, it dawned on me that I was speaking Spanish and the clerk was speaking English. I felt a little foolish, but it was fun and checkout went without a hitch.

We flew to Cuenca for a day or two. There we visited a factory. Panama hats are made in Ecuador not Panama. The name resulted because they went to Panama to protect workers building the canal from the sun. All are hand made and take from two days to six months to weave.

After touring Cuenca we flew to Guayaquil and from there to Baltra in the Galapagos Islands. In Baltra we boarded our private cruise ship, The Isabela II. By booking early we were able to get the "Owner's Cabin," one of only three on the lower deck. Our cabin was larger than the cabins on the upper deck. It was near the library, dining room and the lounge. The Captain's office was on one side and the cabin for the ship's doctor on the other. This caused everyone to assume we were special. The Isabela II had twenty cabins, no casino, no shops, no activities and no entertainment. We ate with different people every meal and got to know everyone in the group. Each day we visited one island in the morning. Then came back to the ship for lunch and visited another island in the afternoon. Each evening we discussed what we saw that day and learned about the next day's activities. The midnight buffet was available all night and consisted of self-serve coffee and cookies. The days were strenuous. Nobody in the tour group was awake at midnight.

Each island has a different color sand or lava. The iguanas evolved to be the same color as the island they live on. There were three naturalists on the cruise with us. Ecuador law requires at least one naturalist with every ten individuals on an island. Visitors to an island are limited to designated paths to avoid disturbing the animals. The animals are fascinating. Never having been hunted they have no fear of people. Some seemed as curious about us as we were of them. As we walked along, birds nesting in the middle of the path would ignore us. Sometimes a bird would walk along the path with us. Sea lions sunning or sleeping on the beach acted as though we were not there. The only scary animals were the huge bull seal lions in the water guarding their harems. For such large animals, they had small, not much larger than a room, territories. Let one bull venture into another's territory and you would hear roars of anger all over the island. I think these were just warnings because we never saw any fights.

To celebrate crossing the equator the captain invited the entire tour group to the bridge. We watched the latitude count down to 00.00.00. When we were exactly at the equator, the captain signaled by blowing the ships horn and had champagne brought to the bridge for everyone.

We flew back to Guayaquil and the Hilton Colon Hotel for the traditional Tauck farewell dinner. After dinner, we sat in the bar with Laura and Eileen from our tour group. Lois ordered a grasshopper. Neither the women nor the bartender ever heard of a grasshopper. Lois described how to make them. The bartender must have made extra because when the server brought them to our table he told us how good they tasted.

Sometimes good things just happen by chance. Ten pharmacy schools in the United States and several in Thailand formed a consortium to develop doctoral level programs in Thailand. In Baltimore, I was among the pharmacy faculty invited to speak to a group of visiting deans from Thailand. I was the last speaker before noon and the dean invited me to stay for lunch. Never one to refuse a free meal, I stayed and happened to sit between two of our visitors. We chatted during lunch. I knew several of our faculty went to Thailand for two or three days to talk about their programs. Just making conversation, I offered to go and explain the experiential aspect of our curriculum. They acted interested, but I assumed they were just being polite. A few weeks later I was surprised to receive an invitation to go there the following June. There were more surprises. Lois was also invited and we were going for a month rather than just two or three days. There was an undergraduate student exchange program the same month we would be there. I was not part of the student program but Lois and I would cross paths with the students periodically throughout Thailand. I spoke to pharmacy university faculty, student groups, and various pharmacy and government organizations. In addition, I visited hospitals, health facilities and regulatory agencies. Two students in Thailand expressed interest in Maryland's graduate program. Asked to evaluate their qualifications, I agreed. Was I in over my head? Yes, very much so. How do I interview a potential graduate student for a program I know nothing about? I do not know if I did it well, but I did it.

I was ecstatic and could hardly wait to tell Lois the news. What was to become one of the most interesting experiences of my life came about by chance.

We left Baltimore on an early morning shuttle flight to New York for an afternoon flight on Korean Air. There was a short stop in Seoul, Korea to change planes. There was an anxious hour or two when I thought we had lost a student. We disembarked into a room with two unmarked doors. One exit led to the international area. The other was for those remaining in Korea. All but one of the students chose the door to the international area. We assumed he had followed the majority of passengers and taken the wrong door. Our flight left for Thailand in just over an hour. I was not a chaperone but I could not leave with him still in Korea. One of our students was Korean and explained what had happened in an effort to get someone to locate him. Time was getting short. He had not arrived and I had no idea what to do. He finally showed up at the last minute. The exit that he took led out of the international area. This required him to go through customs, immigration and pay a fee in order to re-enter. I was never more relieved to see anyone in my life.

We arrived in Bankok Saturday about midnight; exhausted after traveling nearly thirty hours. My first meeting was Monday. I was looking forward to just relaxing on Sunday. We got to the hotel and learned there was a meeting after breakfast to review my plans for the week. That's OK; I will still have Sunday afternoon to relax. At least that is what I thought.

At breakfast, both Thai and western foods were available. There were two trays of eggs, sunny side up eggs. One tray had yellow yolk eggs the other orange yolk eggs. Assuming they were from different types of poultry, I asked what the difference was. Communication with the waiter was difficult. The best I could make out was that one tray was out longer than other was. Since I did not know which was which I skipped eggs that morning.

Lunch followed our meeting. Then I learned we were going to visit the Sunday market. Now my afternoon relaxation was out. I would just have to make do by going to bed early. They sold every thing at this market, including birds and dogs. The birds were pets. I never asked about the dogs. That evening, dinner was at a special Thai restaurant. There were very low tables and everyone sat on the floor. Thai's may be able to sit like that but I cannot bend enough. Luckily, there was an opening in the floor for people like me. Everyone from the United States chose that option. This was a wonderful restaurant and included entertainment. Everyone was dead tired. My eyes glazed over periodically. One student fell asleep sitting at the table. Another told me she fell asleep sitting in the ladies' room. This was not the early night as I had hoped. I still had to prepare for the next day. As I was to find out later, this was a typical day. Our hosts were determined to see that we had a good time.

Bankok has two of the top rated hotels in the world. Some we stayed in were out of this world. On the other hand, we refused to stay in two of the hotels that we found unacceptable. The enigma is that the Thais do not seem aware of the difference.

The Thais were great hosts and paid all our expenses while we were there. We traveled by van (when it was just the two of us) or by bus (when we were with the students). There was always an interpreter with us, an absolute necessity once out of the tourist areas. I described our experiential program to faculty at each school and met with several student groups. I visited hospitals and met with hospital administrators and pharmacists to describe the role of practitioners in an experiential program. Their pharmacy society invited me to speak at their meeting of community pharmacists. The community pharmacy group gave me a tie with elephants (symbolic of Thailand) on it. Speaking to a class of pharmacy students later, I pointed to the tie and said, "This is my Thai Tie." There was no reaction. Lois always tells me not to tell a joke when speaking. This goes double when in a foreign country. I expected the trip to be all business. They planned our visit so that much of it was a pleasure trip. We never had to be own our own. A typical day was breakfast at the hotel followed by a speaking engagement and lunch. Another meeting in the afternoon and, time permitting, a visit to a cultural or pharmacy related site. Dinner would be at a restaurant, sometimes with entertainment, often hosted by someone who I met during that day. It was tiring but fun.

Most people receive medical care in a hospital rather than from a private physician. We visited a hospital with a 105% occupancy census. This meant five people were sharing a bed with another person. Most of the pediatric patients were suffering from dysentery due to the poor water quality. Families usually accompany the patient and help with his care. There were hundreds of people in a huge waiting room. There were water coolers with drinking water. However, instead of paper cups there was a single metal cup attached to the cooler with twine. Their rubber gloves were not disposed of after use but washed, hung in the sun to dry and reused. It was incongruous; the sophisticated technology was up to date but the simpler, public health issues lagged far behind.

When not scheduled to speak and while traveling our guide took us taken sight seeing. We saw so much that we would never have seen otherwise. We saw the "touristy" sites, but we also had experiences missed by those on the tours.

We visited one of the "floating markets" on a canal about an hour from Bankok. Farmers brought vegetables from their farms to sell from their canoes. There was a pavilion built over the water. The bathrooms emptied directly into the canal. I suspect that more was floating in that water than boats. Farmers washed their vegetables and people washed their babies and themselves in this water. No wonder the hospital was full.

We left Bankok on a bus with the students, two of who were suffering from the Thai equivalent of Montezuma's revenge. As we were leaving, our guide told us that the bathroom on the bus was not functioning. We should not worry. If a bathroom is needed the driver will find a nice place to stop. That did not happen. When Montezuma calls, there is no time for searching for a nice place. I saw some of the most god-awful rest rooms ever. Fortunately, I never needed one. Unfortunately, Lois did.

Kanchanaburi is infamous for the "death railway" and its POW camp. This was the setting for the (highly inaccurate) movie, "The Bridge on the River Kwai." A bamboo hut where the prisoners lived is a museum and memorial to the men who were forced laborers there. Actual pictures of the camp from WWII displayed inside are horrific. Over 100,000 soldiers died building the railway during 1942-1943. From the pictures and displays, it is a wonder that anyone survived.

Photographs cannot be taken inside the hut. The bridge over the river, originally built of wood, is still there but is now metal.

After visiting the university in Chiang Mai, we visited an elephant training camp in the jungle. They gave us bunches of bananas to feed to the elephants. The elephants did not want just one and would grab the whole bunch when they could. The elephant ride was a real experience. I sat with Lois on the bench; the trainer sat cross-legged on the elephants head.

The trainer did not speak English but motioned me to come up and sit where he was. I do not bend enough to sit cross-legged so I straddled the elephants' neck. The guide got off, motioned for our camera and took our picture. This was a very narrow trail on the side of a steep hill. The trainer was nearby but not paying much attention. I don't speak Thai or elephant. What do I do if he starts going the wrong way? I don't even know what the right way is. If he decides to head into the jungle, I do not know how to say, "whoa!"

Nearby we could see into one-room shacks that passed for houses as we walked by. I assume they were for the employees. All were a jumble of pots, pans, clothes, etc. Several had marijuana growing in flowerpots.

This trip also led to one of the few battles I had with the School of Pharmacy. The consortium requested that those coming from Maryland all arrive on the same flight to simplify picking us up at the airport. I agreed to coordinate this and to go through UMAB's travel agency. I did and got the airline prices through them. One of my students was from Thailand and went there regularly. She suggested Korean Air for the best rates. I compared prices and found I could save about $1,000.00 on each ticket. Upon my return, I submitted my travel receipts and waited. Each time the money was not in my pay, I called the business office. Each time I was told, "It is in process." Finally, someone told me my request was lost. Now I would have to resubmit my receipts. Now this is months later. I did not have any duplicate copies. They were sorry, but they could not reimburse me without receipts. I remember that Thursday quite vividly. I rarely argue, but there is a limit to my patience and I reached it. As best as I remember I said, "I'll tell you what. I worked hard and saved the university about $5,000.00 on this trip. I am going to hang up. When I do, I am leaving for home. I am not coming back until you find a way to reimburse me." The following Monday I received a call saying that I would get my money. Somebody found a way. I went back to work on Tuesday.

I was a volunteer for the American Heart Association Maryland Affiliate. Two physician brothers, one president of the Maryland association and the other president of the Irish Cardiac Society began a series of yearly meetings alternating between the two countries. This meeting was in Dublin. There were fifteen-minute segments allocated to participants to speak. I used my fifteen minutes to tell about a pharmacy program under development at the Maryland Association. The real purpose of the speeches was to qualify the meeting as a business expense so a portion would be deductable.

Don, Michaeline, Lois and I decided to go together. We spent a few days in London. Then rented a car and drive to Dublin and back. We would see the sights along the way. I preferred that Don drive us out of London because he had driven there before and had some familiarity driving on the left side of the road. Once we left London, we took turns driving. We watched out for each other, calling attention to the direction the cross traffic would come from, etc.

We stayed overnight just outside the city of Bath, England. In the morning, we took a taxi into the city. The driver was very friendly. It was the middle of rush hour. The driver pulled to the curb just after we crossed a bridge. We got out. There were shops on the bridge itself. Their storage rooms are beneath the shops in the stone bridge supports. The driver wanted to show us the windows in the bridge supports that provide light in the storage rooms. We blocked an entire lane of traffic. No horns blew and no one seemed to mind. Imagine blocking a lane of traffic on Pratt Street during rush hour. In the taxi on the way back to our motel, we told this driver that we were from Baltimore. He said, "What a coincidence, I had people from Baltimore this morning." We just happened to get the same cab and driver that we had that morning.

After leaving Bath and on our way to the ferry, we stopped at Stonehenge. The rocks are immense. They were moved a incredibly long distance and set up here without the aid of machines.

We continued through Wales and took the ferry to Ireland. Waterford is not far from the ferry terminal in Ireland. We arrived on a bank holiday so the Waterford Company was not open. We decided to continue, rather than lose a full day of travel. Lois and Michaeline thought this was unfortunate. Donald and I thought we saved a lot of money.

There was a lot to see on the way to Dublin. If something appeared to be interesting, we stopped. We passed the Syntex Pharmaceutical Company and dropped in. They welcomed us and gave us a tour of the facility.

We stopped at a small castle in the process of restoration. At the locked door, we found a note that said, "See Jim for a tour" and gave a nearby address. We found Jim at his home. He gave us a key, and an obviously used brochure but no tour. Jim asked us to return the key when we were done.

Another couple arrived as we were leaving. We gave them the key and the brochure and asked them to return it to Joe. After that, we referred to this as Mr. Jim's castle.

We stayed at a very nice hotel in Dublin. We did some sight-seeing and attended the meeting where Don and I gave our talks. Following the meeting, we went to dinner and a comedy show. Everyone in the audience laughed continuously; we seldom seemed to understand why. It must be that the Irish sense of humor is much different from ours.

The meeting was in Dublin, our last stop in Ireland. We waited in line for the ferry to take us back to England. When the time came to drive onto the ferry, the engine would not start. I told an attendant of our dilemma. He said, "Don't worry we will push you onto the ferry. I asked, "What about getting off?"

His response, was "Don't worry, they'll tow you off." We were the last car off the ferry. The passengers were and the ferry was on the way back to Dublin. The employees were gone and the buildings locked. We were there alone. Now what? Luckily, Don found a pay phone and called Rescue Service, the English equivalent of AAA. Then we waited. The Rescue Service man arrived before too long. He asked what the trouble was and I told him, "The car won't start." After one glance at the car he said, "I know what the problem is. Let me get a piece of wire." This had something to do with the radio. The wire would bypass the problem. The car started immediately and ran trouble free the rest of the trip. How did he know?

Upon leaving the Ferry terminal, we made a last minute change in plans. Instead of driving directly back to London, we made a side trip to Chester. We stopped in antique store in Chester. Lois bought a piece of Wedgewood and I bought an old pharmacy citrate of magnesia bottle.

Michaeline always checked out the hotels in her Foder's guidebook well before we arrived and made reservations. Since this was not preplanned, we had no reservations. I stopped at the first hotel we came to. Other than being old, there was nothing wrong with it. Michaeline did not care for it. She looked through her Foder's guide and picked another. Donald called and made reservations. One of us, me I think, chose the wrong address from the guidebook and we ended up at the wrong hotel. We knew we were at the wrong place but this one was very elegant. Donald cancelled the earlier reservation and we spent the night in this very expensive alternative. I am glad that we did. I never stayed in a nicer place. Dinner was superior. Pre-dinner drinks, desserts and coffee were served in what looked like a living room. The dining room and the food were exquisite. Dessert and coffee was in the living room.

The bellhop appeared to be about ninety years old. Don and I helped him in and out with our luggage because we were afraid he would have a heart attack carrying all our stuff. From here, we drove to London, stopping in Stratford on Avon along the way.

The final adventure was trying to return our rental car. Don and I left Michaeline and Lois at the hotel lounge. As we arrived at the airport, we found about a dozen rental car agencies located side by side. Our first stop was the wrong company with a similar name. Then we drove past the rest of them, turned around and drove by them again without finding the one we were looking for. A cab driver we asked was no help. Back at the airport, we stopped at a car rental agency and asked for directions. The agent claimed not to know where our car agency was located. He suggested we look for a shuttle bus with their name on it and follow that. We made another trip through and a mile or so beyond the airport. Finally, there it was. We returned the car, but forgot to tell them about the car not starting or the wire patch that fixed it. I hope the car worked for the next renter.

Lois and Michaeline were worried because we were gone so long. However, they had an adventure of there own. A man offering to buy them drinks occupied them. Michaeline was leery and ignored him. Lois thought this was an overreaction and amusing. He seemed pleasant so she talked to him.

Lois and I always tell our friends not to invites to visit you unless you mean it. Lois's sister Carole and her husband Tedd were living in Linz, Austria where Tedd was working. Never one to turn down an invitation to travel we packed up and left to spend two weeks with them. The flight was inexpensive because our son, Douglas, worked for Pan Am World Airways. Douglas brought his boss to meet us while we were waiting to board. We spoke for a few minutes. His boss walked to the ticket counter, came back and said, "I was able to get you upgraded." Not only were we going cheap, we were going first class. We had drinks while everyone else was boarding. Dinners, selected from a menu, were excellent and elegantly served. The seats reclined so that we actually slept comfortably. In the morning, there were hot towels so we could freshen up and a very nice breakfast. First class is the way to go.

Tourist destinations, especially in large cities, are pretty much the same around the world. Staying with Tedd and Carole made this a much different experience than a typical foreign vacation. Although we did the touristy things, experiencing daily life in Austria was the real fun.

The local restaurants were different. No, "Please wait to be seated" sign, everyone seated himself. Rolls were already on the table in a basket along with a container of bacon fat in place of butter. The waiter would bring butter when we asked for it, but seemed to wonder why. When ready to leave the server asked how many rolls we ate, and sometimes even what entrees we had, then completed the check. At a pizza restaurant, there was a menu with over a hundred options. You chose the pizza by number. I never thought to remember my pizza's number and was at a loss when the waiter asked what I had so he could write the check. I had no idea. I think I just picked a number at random. When leaving a restaurant, it is customary to say goodbye (wiedersehen) to the diners.

When we arrived at Tedd and Carole's apartment, we met a young teenager who lived in the same building. Carole introduced him; he talked with us and apologized for his poor English. His English was better than that of most teenagers in Baltimore City. I knew that almost everyone in a city of any size spoke English, but I memorized a number of phrases in German because I think it changes the relationship if an American tries to speak the native language. I made it a point to say, "Ich bin ein apoteke auf der USA" whenever I went into a pharmacy. This always started a conversation, in English, with the pharmacist or clerk. It was a challenge to try to buy things speaking in German. I know almost all clerks spoke English and they knew I was an American. Some played along while others just switched right to English.

Tedd worked during the week. Carole was an excellent tour guide. The cathedrals in Austria are tourist attractions and are unbelievably huge and extremely ornate. St. Florian was one of about thirty cathedrals that Carole wanted us to see. Anton Bruckner, an Austrian composer, is buried in St Florian. Carole and Tedd were never able to find his resting place. A tour group was at the front of the church when we arrived. You would have to be there to appreciate just how far away they were. Suddenly, they were gone. Carole said, "I bet they're going to see Bruckner, we should follow them." We went up the aisle, past the altar, through a doorway and down a flight of stairs. We reached the floor below and met a tour group coming up from an even lower floor. Their guide said, "Yes, Bruckner is buried down there." Down we went into the catacombs. It was very dark and dingy. The light came from a few bare bulbs strung along the ceiling. Along both sides of this immensely long church were alcoves with ornately carved coffins and large marble statues. We reached the far end of the catacombs and caught up with a tour group. Bruckner's coffin was in the center. The guide spoke French so we did not understand anything he said. The tour group left, we stayed. The entire end wall was stacked from floor to ceiling with skulls and skeletal bones that came from the cathedral cemetery during an expansion. Leaving Bruckner's burial place, we began working our way back toward the entrance. Suddenly, the lights went out and we heard a gate clang shut. It was impossible to see anything. Lois screamed. Carol and I said nothing for a split second, and then yelled, "Wait we're still down here." A few seconds later, the lights came on and we heard the gate open. We ran to the gate. As we walked out, we learned that we should not have been there at all. That lower area was limited to groups with tour guides. The tour that left ahead of us was the last one of the day. Had we not gotten out when we did we would have been there for the weekend. Tedd was more annoyed than concerned. He was concerned because our itinerary for the day changed and he did not know where we were. He was annoyed because he could not understand how we got into this predicament. Ironically, something similar happened to him a few months later.

Matthausen, a World War II concentration camp, is not far from Linz. There are monuments to each of the ethnic groups interred there. Adjacent to the building is the quarry where prisoners got the stones to build Matthausen. On the steps, mid-way between the bottom and top of the quarry, is a landing. Prisoners called it the parachute jump. Guards pushed prisoners over the side from the parachute jump for amusement. Inside is the gas chamber used to exterminate prisoners and the ovens used to burn the bodies. Our visit made the holocaust real. It was very disturbing. Based on Tedd and Carole's advice we decided not to go inside because it is so depressing. I find it unbelievable that people can be this evil just because others are different.

As a child, I took to music lessons just like took to education in general. I agreed with my mother to practice at least a thirty minutes a day. I am sure that I began counting the minutes from the instant I walked in the front door and made certain I never practiced thirty-one. My first lessons were with Edith Yestadt at her home in Overlea. My early approach to music lessons was poor, to say the least. Practice what I was shown, demonstrate it the following week and then forget it. I never memorized chords or scales because no one told me they served any purpose. Had I known they had a purpose it may have made a difference. I switched to another teacher in Overlea but the results were the same. Then, I took lessons from Rudy Killian, a local dance bandleader, for a short time. This might have led to something but there were too many other things going on. I was working, high school was ending, college was beginning, and Lois and I were getting serious. It was just the wrong time.

A number of years after we married, I took a few lessons from Bud, a local musician. He helped me to begin to understand a little about chords and scales. At a Baltimore Lutheran School fund raising auction, I bought twelve piano lessons by their music teacher hoping to learn more about chords and scales. Classically trained, she did not understand exactly what I wanted but agreed to try to help. We worked together and both learned. This helped some. After I began playing with the group that later became Ain't Misbehavin' I took weekly lessons from Lynn Green, another local musician. She was a big help and was teaching me what I wanted to know. However, I was not able to keep up with her lessons and practicing for the band. I still call on her if I have questions. If I had a teacher such as Lynn years ago, I would be a much better musician today.

My first experience playing in a band was during high school in a small dance band. We practiced in my parents' living room because I had the piano. I think the only reason my parents tolerated the noise was that they knew where I was and what I was doing. Our first gig was at the Overlea Recreation Center. We were so bad that Larry bought beer during a break. I doubt that we played any better, but the beer either made us think we did or we no longer cared how bad we sounded. We played a party on New Year's Eve, but were unable to collect our pay. Chanel 13 (then WAAM) had a TV talent show. An American Legion Post sponsored us so we chose "The Legionnaires" as our name and played "Shanty Town." Listeners chose the winner by sending in post cards. We mailed in lots of post cards voting for ourselves. It was not enough because we did not win. We were all in the same class so when high school ended we went our separate ways and the band disbanded.

One evening, I answered the telephone and heard, "This is a voice out of your past." It was Jim Coffman. Maurice, Jack and Jim, all played saxophones in our high school and were getting together in Jim's apartment every Thursday night. This was just for fun. They would have a few drinks and play some music. Jim invited me to join them. The musicians from high school together again.

Jim had no piano. The first few weeks I used a mini-keyboard Douglas had as a child. Sometimes the music called for notes lower or higher than on the short keyboard. That was very disconcerting. I bought a real keyboard. Soon we added a trumpet.

When we added a few more musicians, it became necessary to move all the furniture out of the living/dining room into Jim's bedroom. When a drummer joined, we had to find a larger place to practice. We bounced around several different places. A customer in Jim's snack bar who was a musician told Jim he remembered how difficult it was for his band to find a place to practice. He offered us the use of space in his packaging business after hours. He gave Jim a set of keys and the alarm code. Not many people would be willing to allow strangers unsupervised access to their place of business. He was very trusting, a good way to be. His packaging business slowed and the owner needed to rent the space we used. Now we were looking again. Gordon Thomas, our guitar player, found us a permanent home at the Maryland School for the Blind.

The Wilson Point Men's Club in Middle River invited us to play. We needed a name. Until then no one even thought about it. We tried but never came up with anything appropriate. One night we practiced a new arrangement, Fats Waller's, 'Ain't Misbehavin''. Someone suggested Ain't Misbehavin' would be a good band name. That became the band's name and our Ain't Misbehavin' became our theme song.

The following year we played for the Wilson Point Community Association beach party. We were now playing real music for real people.

Ain't Misbehavin' grew. Eighteen musicians regularly showed up for practice each week. We reached big band size and could play full big band arrangements. We had requests to play for retirement homes, charity affairs, club functions, awards banquets, etc.

A number of our charts are the original arrangements. I like to put on a CD of a band such as Glenn Miller or Count Basie and play along with Moonlight Serenade or April in Paris. No one in the band is playing for money. Gigs are not jobs. Playing is fun. It is rewarding to hear an audience react when they recognize a tune or see to see a couple in the audience get up and dance in the aisle. Ain't Misbehavin' is a long way from the high school band and from our beginning in Jim's living room.

The Liberty Ship John W. Brown is an operational, World War II Memorial and Museum. My grandfather helped build liberty ships at the Bethlehem-Fairfield shipyard during World War II. He took me there to watch a ship christened and launched. Ain't Misbehavin' played on the liberty ship John W. Browns Veteran's Day Memorial Cruise in November 2007. The John Brown halted at Ft. McHenry for a ceremony to remember all those who sailed on liberty ships during World War II. Our trumpeter sounded Taps as a wreath dropped overboard. It was a very moving experience.

This was a very windy, bitter cold day. The band played on the forward hatch cover where there was little protection from the wind. I shivered the entire time and my fingers nearly froze. Blowing on them and putting them in my pockets between songs did not help. During each short break, we went inside to get coffee in an effort to warm up. Holding the hot cup in my hands helped more than drinking it. As we packed up everyone complained about the cold. More than a few said, "I'll never do this again."

The following spring we were invited to play on the John W. Brown the following October. Everyone in the band said they wanted to do it. This time we played appropriate music for a series of events during a day long "Living History Cruise." Events that happened during World War II were re-enacted throughout the cruise. Abbott and Costello, Rosie the Riveter and other re-enactors appeared. As President Roosevelt and his party came aboard, by cargo net in his wheelchair, we played Ruffles and Flourishes and Hail to the Chief. When General MacArthur approached the microphone to speak, we played the army Caissons Song. At appropriate times, we played a medley of armed forces theme songs, 1940's era music and songs appropriate for each particular event. There was an air show. The ship was "attacked" by Japanese Zeros and a dive-bomber. The Armed

Guards fired back. In the end, an American P-51 drove them off. A B-25, often used to protect convoys, flew above the ship.

My memoirs are about complete except for editing. It is November 6, 2008 and I am doing that now. The Veterans Day Memorial Cruise for 2008 is tomorrow. They invited Ain't Misbehavin' to play again this year. Despite what we all said last November, everyone is in favor of playing. It appears the weather will be a little nicer.

The history of the liberty ships and those who sailed them during World War II is gripping. Prior to our direct involvement in World War II, liberty ships carried cargo to our European allies. Once the United States became involved in the war, they transported our troops, prisoners of war, and cargo. The enemy ruled the seas early in the war. Liberty ships left port with no guns or escort protection. Congress could not authorize placing guns on cargo ships because of the 1939 Neutrality Act. The act was repealed (November 1941) and guns and Navy Armed Guard crews were added. Submarines sank liberty ships within sight of the U.S. coastline. Survivors remember lights that lit up the shoreline from Texas to Maine. Outlined against the glow of lights from businesses afraid they would lose customers, the ships were sitting ducks for German submarines.

The sailors were merchant seaman who volunteered. The only military on board were the armed guards. The armed guard's orders were "to continue to fire their guns as long as the ship was afloat" in order to protect the crew and prevent the cargo from falling into the hands of the enemy. Casualty rates were extremely high. The armed guards and crew may be the least recognized heroes of World War II. I was not surprised when I learned that the liberty ships had the highest casualty rate of any military unit in WW II. It is worthwhile to make the trip to Locust Point and visit the John Brown or take one of their Living History Cruises.

Touch of Class is Boumi Shriners dance band that includes several of the same musicians and plays much of the same music as Ain't Misbehavin'. I substituted for their regular pianist when he became ill.

After he died, they asked me to continue. During 'closed' meetings, I left the room when the business session was in progress. I am not much of a joiner of organizations. However, I felt I should belong to the shrine if I was going to play regularly. In order to become a Shriner, I had to become a Mason first. In January 2007, I became a Mason and shortly thereafter, a noble in the Ancient Arabic Order of the Nobles of the Mystic Shrine (AAONMS). I was a shriner.

In September 2007, Touch of Class played in the Shrine band competition in the Convention Hall at Virginia Beach. Touch of Class received a "Superior" rating, the highest possible, from the judges. Two afternoons later, the hotel set up chairs for us and we played on the hotel lawn facing the beach. In front of us, people strolling along the boardwalk stopped to listen. Behind us, in the hotel, couples danced on the hotel room balconies. Not only is playing great fun, it is very gratifying.

Sunday, as I was leaving, a couple getting on the elevator saw my equipment and realized I was with the band. They asked how we did in the competition. I said, "A Superior." The man said, "They couldn't have given you anything less. We were fortunate to be staying in this hotel so we were able to hear you twice more on the beach." Comments such as this make the effort worthwhile.

Although not part of the Boumi marching band, three of us from the dance band joined them on their float in the shrine parade through Virginia Beach. John White, Harry Hall and I wore white pants and borrowed band shirts. John (does not play any instrument) got a baton and pretended to lead. His instructions were, "When the drummer begins his drum roll you begin to lead." Harry (does not play any instrument) played air trombone. He sat in the middle of the float so the judges would not notice. I, who never played anything other than a piano, played one side of the bass drum while the real drummer played the other. The band received an "Excellent" rating in spite of us.

In September 2008, Touch of Class played in the competition

again. This time we received a Superior rating. We had a good time, but the rain and a hurricane warning put a bit of a damper on some activities. We played about four songs on the beach when it started to drizzle. The hotel staff helped us move indoors. They cleared the dining area and we played about two hours for the hotel guests.

Playing in Ain't Misbehaving' and Touch of Class is the best thing that happened to me since retirement. A number of the musicians in Ain't Misbehaving' also play in Touch of class. What a great experience this is. Practice and gigs are fun in both bands. Everyone strives for excellence. However, the only expectation is that you do the best that you can. I am surprised, pleasantly so, that through years of practicing twice a week there has never been an argument. An obvious mistake is likely to result in a sarcastic comment. However, there are never any hard feelings. Everything is in fun and perceived that way. Everyone expects it. No one is exempt. Individuals and sections are recipients. Play particularly well at a practice or a gig and you get positive feedback. Screw up during a gig and you will hear, "Don't worry about it, it happens to everybody." I am not a gifted musician so playing the piano does not come easy. I work as hard to play as I did at any job I ever had. I liked working, but I love playing.

UNANSWERED QUESTIONS ANSWERED

The following are topics or questions from book my daughter Leslie gave me, which I haven't addressed.

What have you accomplished?
Whatever I was responsible for I tried to improve on so that it was as efficient and effective as possible. For the most part, I accomplished that but do not believe it to be particularly noteworthy. That was my job.
I am mechanically challenged. Some time ago my electric drill broke. I decided to take it apart and try to repair it. There was nothing to lose because unfixed it was headed for the trash anyway. I unscrewed everything, poked, pushed and tightened everything I saw and put it back together. I plugged it in, and to my amazement, it worked. Moreover, it is still working. Although not an accomplished musician, I now play in two bands. For me, the last two are real accomplishments.

Did you enjoy reading as a boy?
Yes. I began with comic books. I had a subscription to "Donald Duck" and looked forward to it coming in the mail every month. Comic books may have little or no depth, but encourage kids to read because they are enjoyable and easy to read. Books came later. I particularly remember enjoying a series of "Buddy" books. "Buddy on the Farm" and "Buddy..." etc. My grandfather gave me a set of Grolier

encyclopedias. Included was a related set, the "Book of Knowledge." It had encyclopedia type information written as stories. The encyclopedia provided a source for facts, but the Book of Knowledge was enjoyable reading.

What is the nicest thing you ever did for your mother/father?
In 1979, Lois and I gave my parents a 50th wedding anniversary party at the clubhouse in Courthouse Square Apartments where they lived. They were very pleased that so many of their friends attended.

How were your family finances?
I never heard finances discussed. Both my parents were very frugal, probably a result of going through the depression. We were not rich but I never remember wanting for anything.

What was your greatest fear?
As a child, I did not like being alone in the basement of Elmont Avenue at night. The scariest part was walking (actually, I always ran) up the steps dreading that something was behind me.

How far did you have to go to your schools?
I walked about a half mile to Fullerton Elementary and Junior High School. Kenwood High School was about two and a half miles from Elmont Avenue. The school bus picked me about three blocks from home. To get to pharmacy school I walked about a half mile to Belair Road and Overlea Avenue and took the number fifteen streetcar downtown. While Lois was in the X-Ray at University program we rode the streetcar downtown together.

Did you go to ball games as a boy?
Yes. The Baltimore Orioles, in the International League at that time. My father or grandfather would take me to a game now and then.

Both my father and Uncle Louis worked as ushers when Navy played football at the stadium. If assigned to a gate they would telephone home. Then my cousin Ron and I would go to that gate and get in free.

What kind of car did your father drive?
The first car I remember is a 1936 Buick. I can still picture him coming in the driveway with it. I was impressed because it had a real trunk with a spare tire inside.

Do you remember the first meals your wife cooked for you?
The most memorable was the first time Lois made gravy. This was the only time I sliced gravy. Lois took after her mother and became an excellent cook very quickly.

What does it take for a husband and wife to maintain a good marriage?
Two people who love each other and are in love with each other. No effort is required. If effort is required, it is not a good marriage.

What is the gutsiest thing you ever did?
I suppose borrowing money on our home in order to expand the medical equipment business. Lois was concerned but I did not consider it risky. Lois does my worrying for me.

Where do you stand politically?
I am not sure whether I am a liberal republican or a conservative democrat.

What is the best movie you ever saw?
My favorite movie is the comedy, "How to Murder Your Wife," with Jack Lemon and Verna Lisi. This is the only movie I ever watched more than once. Leslie taped it for me.

In what ways are you like your father?
I never thought I was much like my father until I began writing my memoirs. I am very much like him. Character traits such as honesty, truthfulness, punctuality, moral principles, and work ethic, I attribute to my father. Emotionally I am much like my father. When angry, I am more likely to stop talking rather than express it. People rarely know when I am angry. When they think I am angry they rarely know why. Those who assume they know what I am thinking, how I feel or why I did something, are probably wrong. Both parents were frugal. I cannot walk past a coin and leave it on the ground. Before writing a grocery list, I check the trashcan for scrap paper to use. One difference between us is that he found his niche early and I neither had nor wanted a niche. Both my parents kept everything very orderly. I prefer neatness and orderliness but lack the self-discipline necessary to keep things that way.

How do you describe success?
Success is a state of mind; not an event. I am successful for as long as I can continue to answer yes to, "Am I satisfied with the choices I have made throughout my life?"

Do you have a favorite sports team? Why?
Not now. I was a fan of the International League Baltimore Orioles as a youngster and later the Baltimore Colts (of the John Unitas era). The typical professional athlete is an immature, greedy, egotistical, paid gladiator. I like golfers because the concentration is on the sport without the showmanship, etc.

Name three of the most fantastic changes you have seen.
Many fantastic changes occurred during my lifetime as the result of enhanced technology. Good changes occurred in communications (computer, television and telephone) and medicine. I saw great strides forward. Bad changes occurred in communications (computer,

television and telephone) and medicine. I saw great steps backward, the unintended consequences of an over reliance on technology and its overuse, abuse and inappropriate use which has dehumanized communication. E.g,, "Customer Service" is outsourced, to other countries (unfortunate enough) and the customer himself. When I seek help, human providing service is often me.

Which/what was your first pet?
Moonie was actually my grandparents' dog. His mother, pregnant, wandered under our back porch and had her pups. The owner reclaimed the dogs and gave them one of the puppies. My grandfather named him after a comic strip character Moon Mullins because he was so ugly. Moony, of questionable ancestry, was the nicest dog I ever had. My first dog was Patsy, a fox terrier puppy. She chewed on Moonie's ears and he didn't care.

RECOGNITION

I never worked or volunteered expecting recognition. I will say that I am very pleased that others found my contributions worthwhile. I am extremely grateful to those who let me know that what I did was meaningful. This also feeds my ego a little.

Selected for Rho Chi, a national pharmacy honor society
Me, in an educational honor society? That is ironic.

Cumberland Area Health Education Center (CAHEC)
For "diligent support of off campus education"

Maryland Caregiver Program (UMAB School of Pharmacy)
For "Dedication and assistance" to a statewide program for caregivers

Caroline County Health Department
Appreciation "For public presentations" regarding Health issues.

State Advisory Council on High Blood Pressure and Related Cardiovascular Risk Factors. (Governor William Donald Schafer)
I felt it was an honor to be appointed to this committee rather than in appreciation.

Pharm.D. Class of 1996
For "dedication and years of service" as the Director of the Professional Experience Program

American Cancer Society Maryland Affiliate
For volunteer service

Bowl of Hygeia Award (A.H. Robins)
For "Outstanding service to community pharmacy. Awarded to one pharmacist from each state each year.

American Heart Association, Maryland Affiliate.
Rookie of the Year Award
President's recognition award

American Diabetes Association Maryland Affiliate
For "Outstanding service and unselfish aid" in the fight against diabetes

National Association of Retail Druggists Journal
For, "Exemplifying the spirit of community involvement"

Medicine Shoppe International (MSI)
"Good Neighbor Award" for local community programs
President's, Director's and Hall of Fame clubs

Thank you letters
I found sixteen letters from a variety of individuals and organizations expressing appreciation for my services

EPILOGUE

*Anyone who believes you can't change
history has never tried to write
his memoirs*
David Ben Gurion

Is everything I wrote in Memoirs and More accurate? If not perfect, it is as accurate as my memory. Nothing was added or omitted because it was favorable or unfavorable. I wrote what I remembered exactly as I remember it. Dates are as accurate as the sources I found to confirm them.

*The More Things Change,
The More They Stay the Same*
Alphonse Karr

My memoirs begin just after the United States of America ended a decade of euphoric economic growth and a dire economic downturn began. The president when the downturn began was Herbert Hoover, (frequently named among the ten worst presidents) a conservative republican president with a very low approval rating. Elected by a wide margin to succeed Hoover was Franklin Delano Roosevelt, (recently named by academic historians as the third best leader overall) a charismatic liberal democrat. Roosevelt was able to inspire Americans with hope for the future. By the end of Roosevelt's administration the United States and the world had changed for the better.

MEMOIRS AND MORE

My memoirs conclude some seventy years later. The United States of America ended a decade of euphoric economic growth and a dire economic downturn has begun. The president when the downturn began was George H. Bush (frequently mentioned as a candidate as one of the worst presidents) a conservative republican president with a very low approval rating. Elected by a wide margin to succeed Bush was Barak Obama, (too early to rate) a charismatic liberal democrat able to inspire Americans with hope for the future. By the end of Obama's administration the United States and the world had changed...

The future is always an unknown. There is no choice but to wait and see.

"Memoirs and More" took longer to write than I anticipated. However, this has been a most enjoyable endeavor. As I wrote, more and more and more old memories came back to me. I hope you found this as interesting to read as I did to write. If you read something that makes you a better or happier person, even if it me as the bad example, I will be greatly pleased.

From what I learned while writing this, I encourage everyone to write his, (includes women too) memoirs. It is time consuming, but it is not difficult. The sooner you begin, the fresher the memories. You will enjoy doing it and your children and grandchildren will appreciate reading it.

EVENTS TIME LINE

I included a time line because I found it fascinating to associate historical events that occurred not only during the lifetimes of my ancestors but also during my lifetime.

1853	**Benedict Oed Born** (Great-great grandfather)
1854	**Johanna Leonhardt Born** (Great-great grandmother)
1857	James Buchanan elected president
1857	Supreme Court—slaves are not citizens
1858	Lincoln-Douglas Debates
1860	Pony Express
1861	**Philip Dannenfelser, Sr. Born** (Great Grandfather)
1861	Abraham Lincoln elected president
1861	Civil War Begins
1861	Telegraph service begins
1861	Jefferson Davis elected president of the confederacy
1863	**Joseph W. Emge Born** (Great-Grandfather)
1863	Battle of Gettysburg
1865	**Annie Baker Born** (Great-Grandmother)
1865	Lee surrenders, Civil War ends.
1865	Abraham Lincoln assassinated
1865	Andrew Johnson succeeds Lincoln
1865	13th Amendment prohibits slavery
1869	Ulysses S. Grant elected president
1869	First transcontinental railroad
1870	Blacks given the right to vote
1870	**Benedict Oed arrives from Germany**

MEMOIRS AND MORE

1876	Custer and his troops killed at Little Big Horn
1876	Carpet Sweeper
1877	Rutherford B. Hayes elected president
1877	Telephones installed in the white house
1879	Edison invents the incandescent light
1881	James A. Garfield elected president
1881	James A. Garfield assassinated
1881	Chester A. Arthur succeeds Garfield
1883	Brown paper bags appear
1879	**George Henry Oed, Sr. Born** (Grandfather)
1883	**Anna Isabella Redmann Born** (Grandfather)
1885	**Philip Dannenfelser, Jr. Born** (Grandfather)
1885	Grover Cleveland elected president
1887	**Eleanor Emge Born** (Grandmother)
1886	Pharmacist develops Coca Cola
1889	Benjamin Harrison elected president
1890	Zipper
1890	Massacre at Wounded Knee (Chief Crazy Horse killed)
1893	Grover Cleveland elected
1893	Melody for "Happy Birthday" song used for the first time
1894	Hershey Chocolate Bar
1896	The Supreme Court—segregation is constitutional
1897	Bayer Company synthesized aspirin.
1897	William McKinley elected president
1880	Less than 50,000 telephones in the United States
1884	The fountain pen
1896	The Supreme Court—separate but equal is legal
1800's	Hutzler, Hochschild & Kohn, and Hecht built Baltimore's first department stores
1900	Electric vacuum cleaner
1901	Theodore Roosevelt elected president
1903	Wright brothers fly their first airplane
1904	Great Baltimore Fire

MARVIN LEROY OED

1905	**Benjamin (Bernard) LeRoy Oed Born** (Father)
1906	Electric washing machine
1909	William Howard Taft elected president
1910	**Leona Eleanor Dannenfelser Born** (Mother)
1910	Electric toasters
1911	Baltimore completes a sewerage system
1913	Woodrow Wilson elected president
1914	Babe Ruth—International League Baltimore Orioles
1915	Home refrigerators
1917	The U.S. declares war on Germany
1920	The 18th Amendment—prohibition begins.
1920	The 19th Amendment—women get the right to vote
1921	Warren G. Harding elected president
1623	Calvin Coolidge succeeds Warren Harding
1925	GE Monitor Top becomes the first household refrigerator to see widespread use.
1927	Lindburgh flies the Atlantic Ocean solo
1928	Grammar school education mandated
1929	The Panama Canal completed
1929	Herbert Hoover elected president
1929	The stock market crashes—the great depression begins
1930's	60% of U.S. households have refrigerators
1930's	Santa Claus appears in department stores
1930's	Dust storms in mid-west displace 400,000 people
1931	Star Spangled Banner adopted as the National Anthem
1933	Franklin Delano Roosevelt elected president
1933	A storm cut the inlet into Ocean City
1933	Hecht Company features a Toy Town Parade with floating characters
1934	**Marvin LeRoy Oed Born**
1934	Pepsi Cola cost $.05 for a 12 oz. bottle
1934	Hitler becomes Fuhrer of Germany
1934	Nylon stockings

1934	First Donald Duck movie
1935	Social Security
1935	Airplane flights over White House prohibited disturbed President Roosevelt's sleep
1935	The first major league baseball night game
1935	Frank Sinatra on Major Bowes Amateur Hour
1937	Dow Chemical develops plastics
1936	**Carolyn Lois Davidson Born** (Wife)
1939	New York Worlds Fair demonstrates television
1939	Germany invades Poland—World War II begins
1940	Fair Labor Standards Act—40-hour work week
1940	Congress passes military conscription law (Draft begins)
1941	Japan attacks Pearl Harbor. US enters WW II
1942	All branches of the armed forces allow women
1942	Baltimore County Police install two-way radios
1942	Navy plays Columbia in Baltimore (Ticket stub says Marvin's first football Game. Ticket price—$1.50
1944	Birdseye leases refrigerated railroad cars. National distribution of frozen food
1945	President Franklin Delano Roosevelt dies in office
1945	Harry S Truman succeeds Roosevelt
1945	Atomic bombs end World War II
1946	Rationing ends
1948	Number of TV sets in US homes reached one million
1950	Korean War begins
1952	The first Chesapeake Bay Bridge replaces ferries to the Eastern Shore
1952	Baltimore Polytechnic (high school) becomes integrated
1953	Dwight D. Eisenhower elected president
1954	St. Louis Browns baseball team moves to Baltimore
1954	TV begins to replace radio
1954	Baltimore Washington Parkway Opens
1957	**Gregory Davidson Oed Born** (Son)

MARVIN LEROY OED

1957	First Baltimore Harbor Tunnel Opens
1958	**Leslie Davidson Oed Born** (Daughter)
1958	Harundale Mall (Maryland's first enclosed mall) opens
1958	Baltimore Colts beat New York Giants for Championship
1961	John F. Kennedy elected president
1963	John F. Kennedy assassinated
1963	Lyndon B. Johnson succeeds Kennedy
1965	Medicare signed into law by Lyndon Johnson
1966	**Philip Dannenfelser, Jr Died**
1966	The Orioles beat Los Angeles in the World Series four straight games. (I had tickets for the fifth game)
1968	First 911 emergency system
1968	**Eleanor Dannenfelser Died**
1969	Richard Nixon elected president
1970	**Douglas Davidson Oed Born** (Son)
1974	Richard Nixon resigns presidency
1974	Gerald Ford replaces Nixon
1971	The Baltimore Colts win the Super Bowl
1972	E-mail
1973	The second Chesapeake Bay Bridge opens
1973	Baltimore City sells abandoned houses for $1.00 and a promise to refurbish them
1975	**Gregory and Cheryl Marry**
1976	**Danielle Nicole Oed Born** (Granddaughter)
1977	James Carter elected president
1981	Ronald Reagan elected president
1981	Self-monitoring of diabetes becomes the standard of care
1987	Blue Laws repealed in MD. Any business can open on Sunday
1989	George H. W. Bush elected president
1991	World Wide Web introduced
1991	**Benjamin Oed Died**
1993	**Leona Oed Died**

1993 William Clinton elected president
2000 Lucas Koch Born (Step Great Grandson)
2001 George W. Bush elected president
2008 Barak Obama become president elect

GENEALOGY

GREAT-GRANDPARENTS

Benedict Oed (Bernard's grandfather)
Johanna Oed (Bernard's grandmother)
Benedict Oed lived in the village of Baiern, Germany and arrived in Baltimore on August 4, 1870 on the SS Leipzig. Benedict was seventeen at the time, listed his occupation as farmer and traveled in steerage. There was no one else named Oed on the ship. In 1875, he married Johanna Leonhardt. A Heinz and Sophie Leonhardt were also on the Leipzig. It is unknown whether they are family to Johanna.

George Henry Oed, Sr. (Bernard's Father)
Anna Isabella Redmann Oed (Bernard's mother)
I never knew either one. My grandfather died before I was born and my grandmother was in an institution from before I was born until she died.

Philip Jacob Dannenfelser, Sr. (Leona's paternal grandfather)
I never knew my great-grandfather, Philip Dannenfelser, Sr. My grandfather rarely mentioned him so I presume he died before I was born or I when I was very young. My grandfather worked with him in a market and told me that that his father owned a bar.

Joseph W. Emge, (Leona's maternal grandfather)
Joseph Emge was known to me as "Dad Dad" Emge. He owned a broom factory in Baltimore City. Lois has a pendent, apparently

given to him by a manufacturer of broom making machinery. I remember he took two streetcars and a bus from his home on Berwick Avenue near Harford Road to Overlea and then walked to Elmont Avenue to visit with us for several days. He died there during his last visit. If the dates I have are correct, he was 84 at the time. At that age, this was quite a trip, especially the long walk from Belair Road to Elmont Ave.

MATERNAL GRANDPARENTS

Philip Jacob Dannenfelser, Jr.
Eleanor Emge Dannenfelser
My grandmother was Grandma but I called my Grandfather Phil. I have no idea why. Since we don't know our grandparents when they are you we never think of them as children, teenagers or lovers. I have a photograph taken in 1915 when my mother was five and my grandmother twenty-eight. It is a peculiar feeling to see your grandmother as an attractive young woman and your mother as a child.

I knew that my grandfather had a stall in a market at one time. I never knew that he worked there with his father until I inherited a picture of them from my parents.

Although I never heard him talk about playing baseball, I have a photograph of my grandfather in a baseball uniform. A basement closet on Elmont Avenue contained baseball equipment. Although the equipment was obviously very old, it appeared to be of professional quality. The fielders' gloves were much smaller than today's. There was no padding, pocket or web. Players caught the ball in the ball in the palm of the glove. The catcher's mitt was round and about the size of a very large dinner plate. The padding made it almost rigid. There was no web. The ball was caught in a pocket in the center just the size of the baseball. These were the first baseball gloves I used.

MARVIN LEROY OED

Before moving to Overlea, my grandparents lived on Biddle Street. Several other family members lived nearby. The Dannenfelsers moved to the house at 1 Elmont Avenue. The date is not clear but my mother was quite young.

PATERNAL GRANDPARENTS
George Henry Oed, Sr.
Anna Oed
I never knew either of my paternal grandparents. They lived in Highlandtown on Linwood Avenue before moving to Overlea. The Oeds moved into a house at the corner of Kenwood and Greenwood Avenues just a block from the Dannenfelser's house on Elmont Avenue. My grandfather (George Oed, Sr.) operated a grocery store on the first floor of their home. The store may have had a name but I never heard it referred to by anything other than 'the store'. My father lived there with his father, his brother George, Jr. and his sister Thelma. My grandmother, Anna Oed, died in 1962 having spent the last thirty years of her life in Spring Grove Hospital. Her physician said that her problem was hormonal and if the medicines currently available existed then there would have been no need to hospitalize her. Following a home visit, my grandfather threatened to kill himself rather that see his wife returned to Spring Grove. She was, and he did. My father visited her periodically. I went with him occasionally but never allowed inside. My father took over the store and my parents moved from Glenmore Avenue into the apartment above the store.

PARENTS
Benjamin (Bernard) LeRoy Oed
Leona Dannenfelser Oed
My parents were born in Baltimore City, my father on Linwood Avenue in Highlandtown and my mother on Biddle Street in Baltimore City. I know nothing of the early life of either. Photographs show my father's sister (Thelma) and my mother as playmates. They are too

young in the pictures for her to be dating him but I assume this is how my mother and father first met. I never heard many details of their dating or courtship. They married in 1929 and lived in an apartment at Kenwood and Glenmore Avenues, two blocks from Elmont Avenue and one block from *"the store."*